# German Air Force Bombers

of World War Two

Volume Two

by Alfred Price

illustrated by Harold Jacks   John Young

Doubleday & Company Inc, Garden City, New York

Series Editor. C. W. Cain

First published in England, 1969
by Hylton Lacy Publishers Limited,
Coburg House, Sheet Street, Windsor,
Berks, England

## Available in the same series

| | |
|---|---|
| American Fighters | Volume I |
| German Air Force Fighters | Volume I |
| Royal Air Force Bombers | Volume I |
| German Air Force Bombers | Volume I |
| Royal Air Force Fighters | Volume I |
| Japanese Imperial Navy Bombers | |
| German Air Force Fighters | Volume II |
| Royal Air Force Bombers | Volume II |
| American Fighters | Volume II |
| German Air Force Bombers | Volume II |

Doubleday & Company Inc.,
First Edition 1969 Second Edition 1971

Printed in England by Mears Caldwell Hacker Limited, London

# Foreword

VOLUME one of this series described the bombers used by the *Luftwaffe* during its initial lightning victories of 1939 to 1942: the Dornier Do 17, the Heinkel He 111, the Junkers Ju 88 and the Focke-Wulf Fw 200. This second volume is devoted to the second generation of German bombers: the Dornier Do 217, the Heinkel He 177, the Junkers Ju 188, the Arado Ar 234 and the "Mistletoe" pick-a-back aircraft.

Each of the types described in these pages incorporated ingenious design features and, when the sometimes daunting teething troubles had been overcome, was at least as good as its enemy equivalent; in the case of the Arado Ar 234 jet bomber there was nothing in the world that could even compare with it. But, quite apart from its quality, the ability of a bomber to destroy its target depends upon two factors: firstly, the number deployed and, secondly, the strength of the defences it has to penetrate. Never were there more than 150 examples of any of the aircraft described here available for action at any one time. And from 1942 on to attempt to attack targets in Great Britain by day or by night was to court swingeing losses, as German units discovered when they tried it; by the summer of 1944 the same powerful defences seemed to stand guard over almost every important target the Germans wished to hit.

None of the types described here can be labelled as "great", for none of them accomplished great things. But greatness and quality are not necessarily linked, and as the successors of the bombers which were the terror of Europe in the early war years these aircraft have a well-deserved place in aviation history.

I should like to thank Franz Selinger, John Taylor, Phillip Moyes, Richard Seeley and Eddie Creek for allowing me to use photographs from their superb collections, also David Irving for help with the text and Richard Smith for checking the manuscript. Once again I should like to wish *"Hals- und Beinbruch!"* to the ex-*Luftwaffe* members who spared me their time to recount the stories repeated here; listening to their experiences has been almost as exciting as living through them—and certainly less dangerous!

*Tickhill, August 1968*

*Alfred Price*

# Contents

Arado Ar 234                     5
Dornier Do 217                   15
Heinkel He 177 Griffon           28
Junkers Ju 188                   44
The Mistletoe                    50

*Colour Illustrations*

Arado Ar 234B                    7/10
Dornier Do 217K-2                17/18
Heinkel He 177A-5                31/32
Heinkel He 177A-5                39/40
Junkers Ju 188A                  41/42
Junkers Ju 188E                  55/56
Mistletoe 2                      57/58

# Arado Ar 234

The Arado Ar 234 Lightning*, the world's first jet bomber, was the great white hope of the German bomber force during the final year of the war. Here at last was a machine which could outrun the fastest interceptors, and penetrate the strongest defences. Had the war continued into the autumn of 1945, it was planned to equip a major part of the bomber force with the type.

But it was not to be. In the event only 214 of these advanced aircraft were built, and such was the confusion at the end of the war that little over half of them ever saw action.

There can be no doubting the importance which Hitler attached to the production of jet bombers. In

*Blitz

the diary of Albert Speer, Hitler's armament minister, one finds the entry of June 22, 1944:

"The Fuehrer orders again, in a meeting with the Reich Marshall*, his unalterable demand for the immediate peak production of jet bombers. Until the series production of the 234 can be secured as the final aim, the series production of the 262 is to be pressed on with all speed, and must be made available for this purpose†. In order to have this demand satisfied a forced drive will have to be

*Goering

† This use of the Messerschmitt Me 262 jet fighter as a high-speed fighter-bomber was a major error since the type achieved little in the role, and moreover it prevented the jet fighter being used against the Allied bomber formations where it might well have caused serious losses. See German Air Force Fighters of World War II, Volume One, in this series.

carried out with much more energy than hitherto applied, by energetically concentrating on . . . procuring all needs such as to quotas, bottlenecks of materials (especially nickel), machinery and labour, and simultaneously securing underground production . . ."

Such was the urgency of the programme that Hitler specifically decreed that the Ar 234 was to go into action at the earliest possible moment, even if this meant that service pilots would have to observe maximum speed and stress limitations at first.

## DEVELOPMENT

The Ar 234 was designed to a 1940 German Air Ministry specification which called for a single seat, jet-propelled, high speed reconnaissance aircraft, and the prototype made its first flight from Rheine near Muenster on June 15, 1943.

The airframe of the new aircraft was conventional in all but one respect: the landing gear. In place of the more usual wheeled undercarriage—which had been omitted to allow more space for fuel—the early prototypes employed a jettisonable trolley for take off and retractable skids for landing. The trolley system worked well enough during the flight trials. But it was judged too be to cumbersome for large scale service use, because after landing the aircraft would all have to be hoisted on to their trolleys before they could be towed off the runway; moreover, any aircraft which diverted from its home base would have been helpless until a take-off trolley could be provided.

So the range penalty was accepted and a new subtype with a tricycle undercarriage, the Ar 234B, was built. This flew for the first time in March, 1944. By this time the Arado factory at Alt Loennewitz was tooling up to produce the "B" version in quantity, and the first production types flew in June—when Hitler began his demands for more and more of these aircraft.

Initially the Arados were supplied only to reconnaissance units. But in October, 1944, the only bomber unit to receive the type, Lieutenant Colonel Robert

*An Arado Ar 234B of III./K.G. 76 lets go of a pair of 550 pound bombs during a shallow dive attack. This aircraft was the world's fastest bomber at the end of World War Two, but because it was deployed in only very small numbers it had virtually no effect on the course of the war.*

Kowalewski's K.G. 76 based at Achmer near Osnabruek, started to re-equip with the Ar 234B. For some months previously ground crewmen from disbanded bomber units had been working on the Arado production lines at Alt Loennewitz, helping to produce the jet bomber; now these men were all well qualified to maintain the aircraft in service.

During the early service life of the Ar 234 a few of these aircraft were lost when, after take-off, they rolled on their backs and dived into the ground; in each case the machines disintegrated on impact, and the cause could not be determined. At that stage in the war there could be no question of grounding what was virtually the only effective German long-range bomber and reconnaissance aircraft, and pilots had to face the unknown hazard. Only later was the cause discovered when a pilot of K.G. 76 experienced the fault but, in a demonstration of superb airmanship, managed to roll his aircraft through the full 360 degrees and bring it back to base. With the high pitched vibration of the

*An Ar 234A pictured getting airborne, immediately after it had let go of its take-off trolley. The brake parachute fitted to the trolley is beginning to deploy. Although it worked well enough during trials the use of the trolley for take-offs was judged to be too inflexible for large scale service use, and subsequent sub-types were fitted with a conventional undercarriage (Franz Selinger).*

*Above: The eighth prototype of the Ar 234 featured four jet engines in paired nacelles, an arrangement later adopted for the Ar 234C. Note the landing skid arrangement, and the method of attaching the aircraft to the take-off trolley (Franz Selinger).*

Arado Ar 234B flown by Major Hans Georg Baetcher, the commander of the Third Gruppe of Kampfgeschwader 76, from Achmer during the Battle of the Ardennes in the winter 1944/45.

*The remaining views will be found overleaf.*

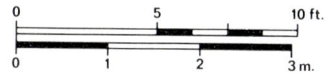

Arado Ar 234B.

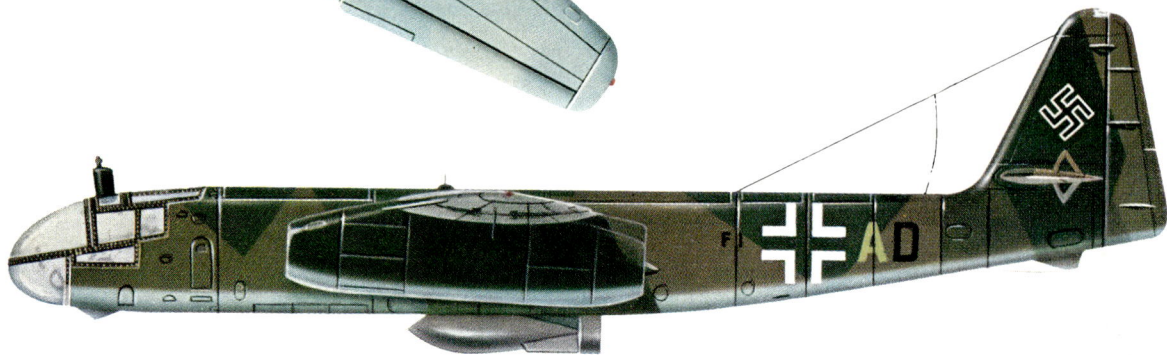

Arado Ar 234B flown by Lieutenant Colonel Robert Kowalewski, commander of Kampf-geschwader 76, from Schleswig, during the Battle of Berlin, April 1945.

*The remaining views will be found overleaf.*

Arado Ar 234B.

jet engines one of the ignitor plugs had unscrewed itself, and blown out. This allowed the searing hot blast from the engine's flame tube to play on the aileron control runs; it burnt them through in an instant, and the aircraft had immediately rolled on to its back. As a result of this discovery the ignitor plugs were tightened up immediately before each flight, and the accidents ceased.

## IN ACTION

The Ar 234 was a small aircraft, and fully loaded weighed about as much as a present-day Hunter fighter-bomber. The maximum bomb load of 3,300 lb. was also comparable with that of the modern aircraft. The Arado's would attack their targets in a shallow dive, or else at low level or high level while flying horizontally.

The form of attack most used was the shallow dive, in which the pilot brought the aircraft down at an angle of 30 degrees at a speed of 600 m.p.h., and used the periscope mounted on top of his cabin to line himself up on the target.

The horizontal low-level attack was also used a great deal; but since there was no low-level bomb sight fitted to the Ar 234 the pilot had to aim his bombs "by eye", a method which tended to be rather inaccurate unless he could make a straight run-in without enemy interference. On March 7, 1945, the Americans seized the bridge over the Rhine at Remagen, and thus breached the last great water barrier and natural defence line in the west. Goering ordered a maximum effort from his bombers to smash the bridge. At the time of the attacks the cloud base was down to 1,500 feet, and Kowalewski was forced to send his Arados in at low level. But in the event the poor weather and the strong defences combined to prevent accurate strikes, and the Remagen bridge survived the attacks.

The high-level attack was used against the more distant targets, for at high altitude the jet engines were far more efficient than they were low down, and the range of the Arado was three times as great. However, this method did have the clear disadvantage that if there was anything more than the most patchy cloud cover, the attack had to be abandoned. If the pilot opted to make a high-level bombing run his work-load was very high, since he alone had to perform the tasks of pilot, navigator, and bomb aimer. Consider a typical high-level bombing attack. First the pilot would line his aircraft up on the target, when some 20 miles from it. He would then engage the three-axis autopilot, *disconnect* the normal control column and swing it to one side. This done he loosened his straps and moved forward to the bomb aiming position in the

*Arado Ar 234 B's.*

11

troops in the Ardennes, solely for this purpose. The U.S. Air Force's reaction was immediate and formidable: standing patrols of fighters at 5,000, 10,000 and 15,000 feet, and when an Arado showed up they all pounced on it. Even so the bombers proved difficult targets, and losses were rare. If the German bombing caused little damage, at least the "decoy duck" tactics tied down large numbers of enemy fighters; it was the nearest thing to air cover the weary German troops were to get during the closing months of the war.

One of the rare occasions when an Arado was shot down while flying at high speed was on March 2, 1945, when Flight Lieutenant John Reid, flying a Spitfire XIV of 41 Squadron, scored a "kill". Reid was patrolling near the Nijmegan Bridge at 10,000 feet when he spotted one of the jet bombers running in at low level. Bravely ignoring the possibility that his over-strained Spitfire might shed its wings, the British pilot pushed his aircraft into a near-vertical power dive and hurtled down after the intruder. He opened fire at maximum range and kept his finger on the firing

Major, later Lieutenant Colonel, Robert Kowalewski commanded Kampfgeschwader 76, the world's first true jet bomber unit (Robert Kowalewski).

nose. The pilot would then look through the eyepiece of the *Lotfe* bombsight, and align the graticule on the target. The bomb sight was connected to the aircraft's automatic pilot via an analogue computer, and the act of maintaining the graticule over the target fed correcting signals to the auto-pilot which in turn "flew" the aircraft throughout the bombing run. After he had released his bombs the pilot would reverse the process and regain his seat.

Obviously the high level attacks would have been quite out of the question if there was any interference from enemy fighters, but for the Arados flying at speeds around 400 m.p.h. at 30,000 feet there was little to fear from that quarter. Kowalewski recalls making one such high level attack on British tanks at Weyl near Dortmund. Dropped from such an altitude the bombs

took almost a minute to reach the surface, during which time the jet bomber had covered some six miles and was well clear. Asked recently whether he had hit the tanks, Kowalewski smiled and replied "*Hoffentlich . . .*"*

Whatever form of attack they chose to use, so long as they kept up their speed, the Arado pilots had little to fear from enemy fighters. For this reason the jet bombers were used on a number of occasions as bait, to draw Allied fighters away from more profitable ground targets. The commander of III./K.G. 76, Major Hans Georg Baetcher, recalls that his unit made several single-aircraft nuisance raids on American

*"I trust . . ."

*Captain, later Major, Hans Georg Baetcher (centre, in the light cap) commanded the Third* Gruppe *of K.G. 76. He is seen here during the celebrations following his* five hundredth *operational sortie, while commanding the He 111 unit III./K.G. 100 in Russia. Baetcher ended the war with* six hundred and fifty eight *operational sorties, probably more than any other multi-engined bomber pilot in the world. These sorties are authenticated in his log books. Such a total might seem unbelievable to British or American readers, but it should be remembered that in the Luftwaffe there was no such thing as a "rest" job between operational tours. Aircrewmen flew on operations until they were killed, wounded, or promoted out of the job; the only planned breaks from operational flying were during the men's leave periods. In the light of this a total of 658 operational sorties spread over six years of war is high, but not incredibly so (Hans Georg Baetcher).*

button down to 100 yards when he broke away, leaving the Arado in flames. The German pilot baled out and the jet crashed near Enschede on the German-Dutch border. When Reid landed, his greatly abused Spitfire was fit only for the scrap heap. The fuselage was twisted, and the skinning on the wings had rippled back and was buckled in places.

The only time the Arados were really vulnerable was when they slowed down to land or were actually on the ground. In recognition of this the *Luftwaffe* set up powerful "flak lanes" along the landing approach paths to the airfields. The single barrel 37 mm. and quadruple barrel 20 mm. weapons proved a strong deterrent to fighter attacks within their range. Nevertheless, on April 25, 1945, three Thunderbolts did brave the flak as Major Polletin of *Stab* K.G. 76 was coming in to land. The major was shot down and killed.

When the Arados returned to base short of fuel— and that, Baetcher recalls, seemed to be on every sortie —the rate of fuel consumption at low level was such that the pilots had to go straight in and land as soon as they possibly could. On one occasion he arrived

back at Achmer to find Allied and German fighters dogfighting over the airfield ". . . and the flak gunners, being neutral, firing at everybody!" Baetcher had no alternative but to run in very fast, for a "hot" landing. At the very last moment, and while flying at 250 m.p.h., he extended his undercarriage. At 220 m.p.h. he lowered his flaps and at 175 m.p.h. he forced the protesting aircraft down on to the runway. As soon as the wheels were firmly on the ground, Baetcher streamed his tail brake parachute. But even so this harsh treatment proved to be too much for the synthetic rubber on the port main wheel, which promptly blew out. The aircraft lurched to port off the runway, and Baetcher was treated to a high speed run across the grass before man and machine came to rest a little shaken, but otherwise little the worse for the experience.

By 1945 the part of Germany remaining under Nazi control had shrunk to such an extent that Osnabruek was threatened and K.G. 76 was forced to leave Achmer for bases at Luebeck and Schleswig. From these airfields the bombers took part in the final battles on both the Eastern and the Western Fronts, notably the ground actions round Berlin and the Ruhr

areas. At this stage of the war the average Ar 234 bombing sortie lasted only about a half an hour: typically, 15 minutes out, three minutes to attack, and 15 minutes to return.

## NEW DEVELOPMENTS

At the end of the war several developments of the Ar 234 were either flying or about to fly.

The C sub-type, with four BMW jet engines instead of the two Jumo units on the Ar 234B, was in full production when the end came and was on the point of entering service. It was somewhat faster than the B, and later versions were to have had a two-man crew comprising a pilot and a navigator.

The war ended before the 16th prototype of the Ar 234 could make its first flight. This machine, which was to have been used for aerodynamic research, featured a crescent-shaped wing similar to that later fitted to the British Victor bomber.

*Refilling the forward fuselage tank on an Ar 234B. The low grade fuel used by the jet engines was the only type not in critically short supply in Germany during the closing months of the war.*

*The Ar 234C featured four jet engines, and this example had an enlarged cabin to house the two-man crew (Franz Selinger).*

Another interesting idea which was actually tested was the use of a rigidly towed V1 flying bomb, without a warhead, as a fuel container to extend the range of the Ar 234. As in all matters concerning this aircraft Hitler's interest was great, and the entry dated November 5, 1944, in Speer's diary recorded:

"Reported to Hitler on the experiments intended with the 234: to employ it as a valuable super-fast warplane, by rigidly connecting it with an engine-less V1 weapon and using the fuel container of the V1 as an additional tank for the outward journey, so as to give the 234 the widest possible range and to enable it to carry a considerably heavier external bomb load. Hitler expects these experiments to be concluded with all possible speed and tested in practice."

*The only time the German jet aircraft were really vulnerable to enemy action was when they were landing, or actually on the ground. To discourage attacks, scores of these quadruple barrelled 20 mm. automatic anti-aircraft weapons guarded the German airfields and the approach lanes to them (Imp. War Mus.).*

During these trials the tailplane of the V1 was removed altogether, as was the pulse-jet motor. To enable the carcass of the flying bomb to be towed off the ground, it was fitted with a simple fuselage-mounted two-wheel undercarriage. The war ended before the system could be used operationally.

When the end came the Arado Ar 234, the wonder of its enemies, had still to make a tangible mark on the course of the war. The decisive air battles had all been lost or won by pilots flying "conventional" aircraft. If the war had continued for another year the jet bomber would have seen large-scale service. But if the war had continued for another year the Allies would have had jet fighters in service in large numbers to counter the menace, and the German bomber units would have had to face the same swingeing losses as they had when flying piston engined aircraft.

## SPECIFICATION Ar 234B

**Crew**
One.

**Power plant**
Two 1,960 lb. thrust Jumo 004B jet engines.

**Dimensions**
Span: 46 ft. 3½ in. Length: 41 ft. 5½ in. Wing area: 284 sq. ft.

**Weight**
Empty 11,464 lb. Loaded 20,250 lb.

**Armament**
Most of the aircraft used operationally by K.G. 76 carried no defensive armament. However a few of these bombers were delivered with two 20 mm. cannon, fixed to fire rearwards and sighted through the rearwards looking periscope mounted on the cockpit roof.

**Maximum bomb load**
3,300 lb., carried externally.

**Maximum speed**
474 m.p.h.

**Maximum range**
1,000 miles, flying at high level.

**Service ceiling**
33,000 ft.

*When the war ended scores of these advanced jet bombers littered airfields all over Germany. This battered Arado was found by the Americans when they captured the base at Manching (via R. C. Seeley).*

# Dornier Do 217

THE Dornier Do 217, which entered service in the spring of 1941, was the first new German bomber type to reach the front after the outbreak of war. During its service career it operated mainly in the west and in the Mediterranean, and achieved the distinction of carrying the world's first guided missiles into action. When production ceased at the end of 1943 a total of 1,730 of these aircraft had been built; 364 were converted into night fighters, and the remaining 1,366 were shared between bomber and reconnaissance units.

The Do 217 was a lineal development of the Do 17 "Flying Pencil"* and was intended as a multi-purpose bomber. The type was stressed for dive bombing, and for speed control during the dive it carried a tail mounted petal air brake.

The first prototype made its maiden flight in August 1938, but crashed one month later. However, two more prototypes had been completed before the end of the year, and the testing programme was resumed. It was the ninth prototype, which flew in the early part of 1940, that became the Do 217E—the first production bomber version. In place of the 1,075 h.p. Daimler Benz DB 601 in-line engines fitted to the first prototype, the E version was powered by two BMW 801 radials each rated at 1,580 h.p. for take off.

*Described in Volume One.

*The first prototype of the Do 217, which flew for the first time in August 1938 (Imp. War Mus.).*

The extra power enabled the sub-type to carry a greater bomb load, and to allow this to be carried internally the fuselage was deepened.

## TEETHING TROUBLES

Very early on in the Do 217 test programme it became clear that the rear mounted petal dive brake was not a success, because when it was extended it placed an excessive strain on the bomber's fuselage. The

*An early production Dornier Do 217E of the anti-shipping unit Kampfgeschwader 40, taxiing out prior to a night sortie. The Do 217 was the first of the new generation of German bombers to enter service after the outbreak of the war. It was a fast aircraft, well liked by crews, but because of the need for simpler bombers on the eastern front it did not see service in large numbers (via P. Moyes).*

Luftwaffe Technical Office* ordered a protracted modification and trials programme in an attempt to overcome the problem. The reason for this insistence upon the aircraft having a dive-bombing capability was that the Germans wanted to be able to bomb with greater accuracy than was possible with their horizontal bombers at that time (later, the *Lotfe* bombsight would give horizontal bombing accuracies as good as those from dive bombers).

In an effort to reduce the stresses on the after fuselage during the dive, a trials aircraft was modified to carry an extra pair of air brakes between the fuselage and the engine nacelles. Each brake was made up of four parallel bars, and during normal flight the bars were in the horizontal, low drag position, clear of the wing. When the aircraft dived the brakes rotated through ninety degrees about the axis of the centre bars, and took up the vertical, high drag, position. To compensate for the severe nose-down trim change which resulted from the use of these air brakes, inter-

*Technische Amt.

15

*The first production bomber version, the Do 217E, entered service early in 1941. This sub-type had a deepened fuselage to accommodate the increased bomb load made possible by the more powerful motors (compare the fuselage shape of this machine with that of the prototype). Note also the long tail section, which comprised the folded petal air brake; a further point of interest on this machine is the additional air brake fitted between each engine and the fuselage (via R. C. Seeley).*

connected trim tabs on the elevators automatically applied a nose-up correction. However the mechanism to achieve this was over-complicated, and following a test dive the elevator trim tabs jammed in the nose-up position; when the dive brakes were returned to the low-drag position the nose of the aircraft rose sharply, and the machine stalled and crashed. The crux of the matter was that the Do 217 was just too heavy to be a dive bomber, and with the realisation of this the petal air brakes were removed from all aircraft delivered as bombers.

## IN SERVICE

The first bomber unit* to receive the Do 217 was the Second *Gruppe* of *Kampfgeschwader* 40†, which

*During 1940 a few Do 217's were employed by reconnaissance units.*

†A Gruppe comprised three Staffeln each of nine aircraft, plus a Stab *(staff) flight of three; it was the basic flying unit in the* Luftwaffe, *and thus was deployed independently in the same way as an R.A.F. squadron. Three* Gruppen, *with an additional staff flight, made up a Geschwader. The* Kampf- *(battle) prefix indicated that the unit operated in the bomber role.*

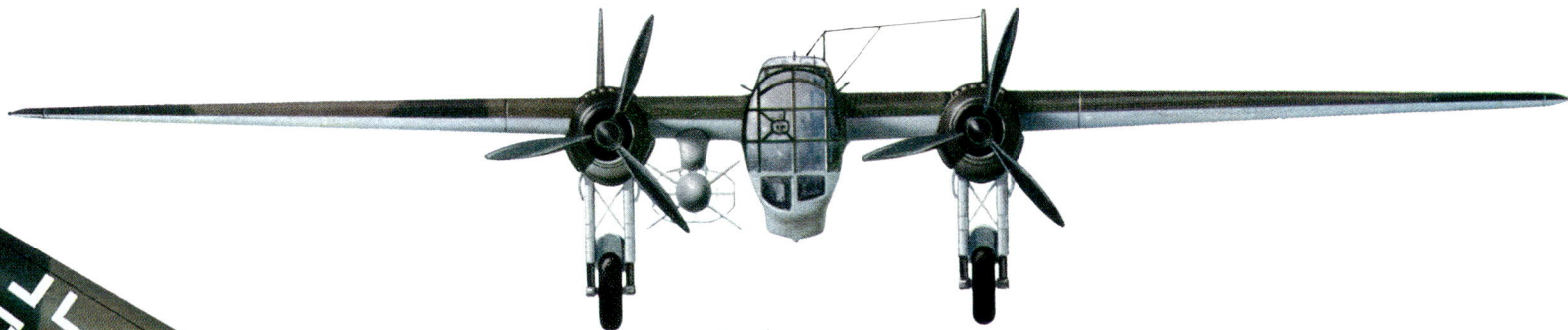

Dornier Do 217K-2 flown by Major Bernhard Jope, commander of Kampfgeschwader 100, from Istres, France, during operations over the Mediterranean in the summer of 1943.

*The remaining views will be found overleaf.*

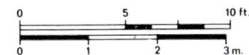

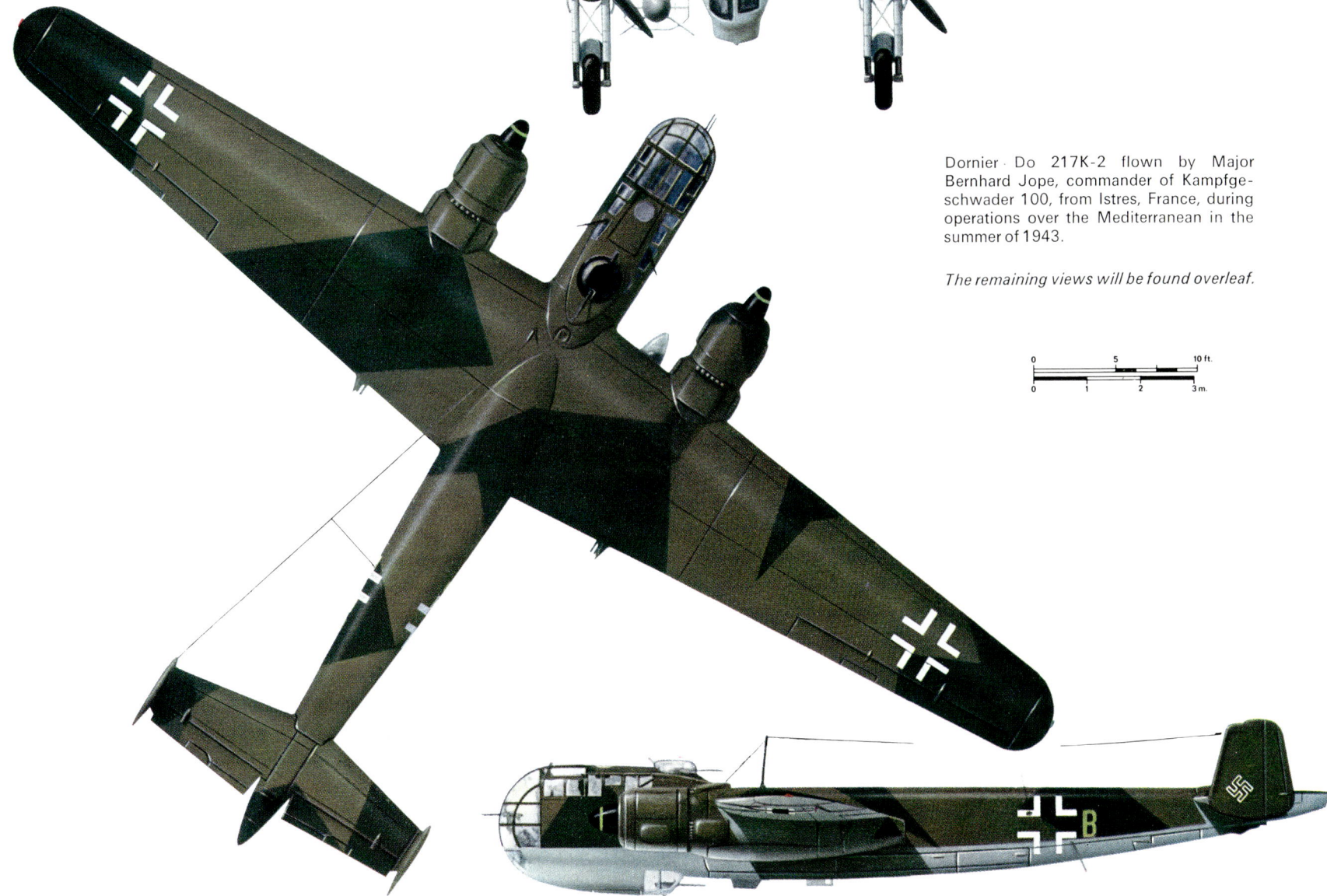

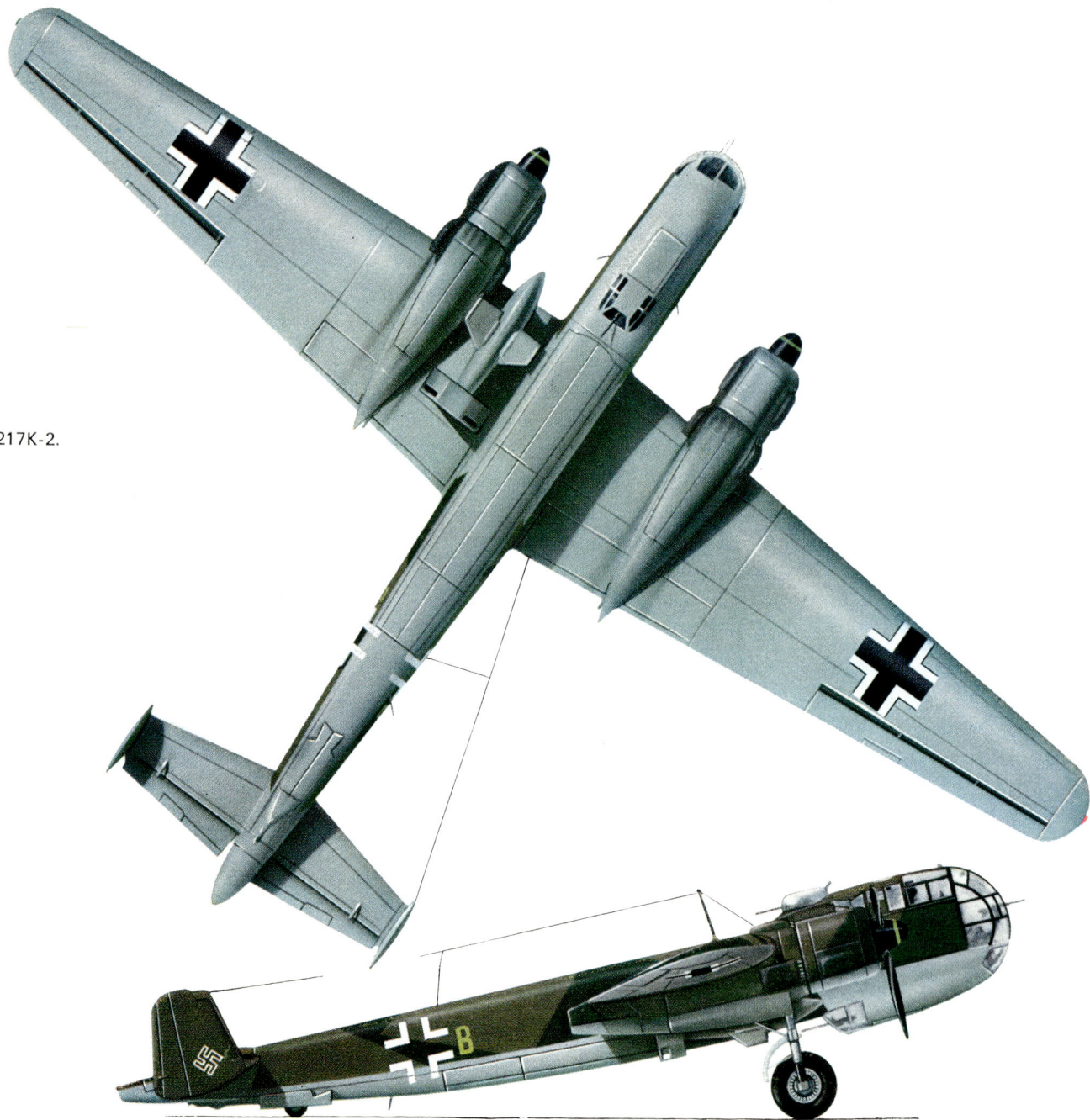

Dornier Do 217K-2.

*This Do 217E, belonging to II./K.G. 2, crashed near Lydd in Kent in October 1941 after being seduced over Britain by "Meacon" spoof beacon transmissions (Imp. War Mus.).*

received its new aircraft in the spring of 1941. The Dorniers operated from Bordeaux/Merignac in France in the anti-shipping role, and carried out armed reconnaissance flights over the Bay of Biscay and beyond. As the year progressed II./K.G. 40 was joined in this task by K.G. 2, as that entire *Geschwader* became operational with the Do 217.

## ONE WAY TO GET A DORNIER

On the October 12, 1941 the Royal Air Force got hold of a Dornier 217, following one of the more bizarre incidents of the war. The aircraft concerned, which belonged to the 5th *Staffel* of K.G. 2, had been out reconnoitering the eastern Atlantic on the evening of the 11th. On the way back to his base at Evreux in northern France the pilot, Lieutenant Dolenga, had strayed a little off course: being somewhat to the north of where he thought he was, he flew up the Bristol Channel instead of the English Channel. So when he crossed the north coast of Devon, he reason-

*Bottom of page 12*
*An early production Do 217E, belonging to II./K.G. 40. Already this aircraft has had its petal air brake removed, and has the shorter tail cone in its place. Note the crudely painted out crosses and fuselage letters, to make the machine less conspicuous at night (R. C. Seeley).*

*Two fine shots of the Do 217K, showing clearly the re-designed all-glazed nose section. This aircraft was flown by the commander of III./K.G. 2 (R. C. Seeley).*

ably took this to be the north coast of Brittany. The error was an easy one to make, and would have been readily apparent when the Dornier's radio compass was tuned in to the German radio beacons in France. But the two beacons used by the Dornier's crew—at Paimpol and Evreux—were respectively covered by the British "Meacon" spoof transmitters at Templecombe and Newbury. The result was that in the darkness Dolenga and his crew crossed the length of

southern England, confident that they were over northern France. When they came to the Thames Estuary the crew took it to be the north coast of France, and accordingly headed southwards towards their home base at Evreux—or so they thought. Imagine then the consternation on board the Dornier when, a few minutes later, the crewmen saw yet another coastline dead ahead! His fuel almost exhausted, the puzzled Dolenga had little choice but

*Above: The Henschel Hs 293 glider bomb, the world's first guided missile to see action, was launched from Do 217's of II./K.G. 100 (U.S.A.F.)*

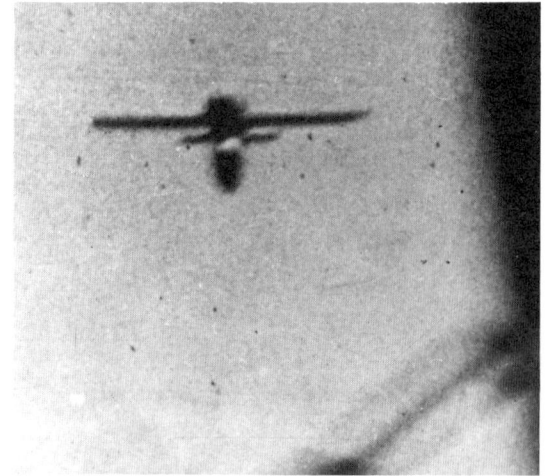

*The receiving end. This remarkable photograph is from a cine film shot by a Royal Navy officer who, with incredible coolness, filmed a glider bomb attack on his ship. The bomb missed—but not by much!*

*Close up of the bomb aimer in the carrier aircraft, seen here operating the radio control unit which transmitted the correction signals to the glider bomb as it sped towards its target (Franz Selinger).*

to set his aircraft down on the open fields below. The machine came to rest at Jury's Gut, near Lydd in Kent.

So it was that the Royal Air Force secured its first example of the Do 217. Some people might argue that wars should be fought by brave men with guns and not like this. But it was one way to get a Dornier.

## THE "BAEDECKER" RAIDS

During the winter of 1941–1942 *Kampfgeschwader* 2, in common with the other German units which remained to fight the holding action in the west, maintained only a desultory effort as it tried to conserve both men and machines. This phase came to an abrupt halt on the night of the March 28, 1942, when a force of 234 bombers of the Royal Air Force razed much of the old German city of Luebeck in a fire attack. The raid caused deep resentment in Germany, coupled with demands for retaliation from Hitler. On April 14 the *Luftwaffe* Operations Staff issued the following order:

"The Fuehrer has ordered that air warfare against England is to be given a more aggressive stamp. Accordingly when targets are being selected, preference is to be given to those where attacks are likely to have the greatest possible effect on civilian life. Besides raids on ports and industry, terror attacks of a retaliatory nature are to be carried out against towns other than London. Minelaying is to be scaled down in favour of these attacks."

The first of the new series of attacks was on the evening of the April 23, when 45 bombers, for the most part Do 217's of K.G. 2, set out to bomb Exeter. The initial attack was a failure but a second raid, by 60 aircraft on the following night, was more successful. On the next two nights the target was Bath, which was badly hit in the raids which together totalled 250 sorties.

But even as the German bombers were pounding Bath, those of the R.A.F. were wrecking the German town of Rostock in a series of four destructive fire raids. Hitler was beside himself with rage when he heard of this development. On the April 26, he made an impassioned speech in which he spoke of taking a copy of Baedecker's guidebook, and marking off each British city when it was destroyed; as a result of this the whole series of reprisal attacks* became known in Britain as the "Baedecker Raids".

Following the Bath attacks Norwich, York, then Norwich again were attacked. In both cities incendiary

*Vergeltungsangriffe.

bombs caused serious fires. During the first of the Norwich attacks early hits by high explosive bombs on the city's water mains resulted in an acute shortage of water with which to fight the fires; as a result 20 factories and many other buildings were gutted. At York salvoes of incendiary bombs fell on either side of the Minster, and straddled the railway lines in the north and north-western quarters of the city; some fifty tons of high explosive bombs struck the centre and the northern quarter. Following a week of continuous action, the Luftwaffe rested for two days. It was preparing for the most devastating of the reprisal raids.

On the night of May 3 the weather was fine and the sky almost cloudless. It was then that the Germans returned to finish the job only half completed at Exeter ten days earlier. This time the target marking was accurate, and the bombers struck hard. Fierce fires quickly took hold of the heavily timbered

The Do 217K-2 featured a longer span wing, to enable it to climb to 20,000 feet when carrying the Fritz-X guided bomb. Note the three posts protruding from the leading edge of each of the wings of this aircraft; these supported the wire aerials of the Lichtenstein S ship-search radar (Dornier).

mediaeval buildings and, unhindered by the narrow streets, raged unchecked until a large part of the city had been gutted.

During the month of May several other lightly defended towns and cities were struck, including Cowes, Hull, Poole and Grimsby. On the 31st of the month Canterbury suffered heavily, if a little less disastrously than Exeter.

Due to the heavy losses at the hands of the steadily improving British defences, the initial fervour of the Baedecker raids fell away rapidly. The dying spasm—three attacks on Birmingham and one on Hull at the end of July—cost the Luftwaffe 27 bombers and caused little damage. Some idea of the cumulative effect of the losses may be gained from the fact that K.G. 2, which had operated over Britain consistently throughout the spring and the summer, lost aircraft and crews equal to its own strength once in each successive three month period. With the failure of the German crew training organisation to make good such losses, the strength of the unit fell to a low ebb: having started 1942 with 88 crews, it had only 23 left by September.

The remainder of 1942 was devoted to resting and refitting the badly mauled Baedecker raiding units,

K.G. 2 included. It was at this time that the next important sub-types of the Do 217, the K and the almost exactly similar M entered service. These versions had a completely redesigned forward section, with a rounded, unstepped cockpit and a fully glazed nose. To safeguard against the possibility of engine shortages two different types of engine were fitted. The K was fitted with the BMW 801D, with the otherwise identical M designed to take the Daimler Benz DB 603 in-line engine. The new versions were some 20 m.p.h. faster than the earlier E.

Early in 1943 II./K.G. 40, which had operated with the Do 217 alongside K.G. 2 in the west, re-equipped with the Heinkel 177; thus for a time the latter unit became the sole operational bomber unit flying the Do 217.

*Do 217K-2's of III./K.G. 100 photographed on the ground at Istres near Marseilles (Jope).*

## GUIDED MISSILES

*Major Bernhard Jope led III./K.G. 100 during the extremely successful attack on the Italian battle fleet (Imp. War Mus.).*

From the beginning of the war the Germans had concerned themselves with the problem of increasing the effectiveness of their aircraft against armoured warships and merchantmen. The long-term answer to the problem, since the aircraft with sufficient range were too heavy to dive bomb, lay in the use of an air-launched weapon that could be controlled from the parent aircraft during its flight to the target. In this way the aircraft could stay out of range of the anti-aircraft fire, but still counter any evasive action the ship might take. Two German firms—the Henschel and the Ruhrstahl companies—each produced a radio guided, anti-shipping weapon.

The Henschel Hs 293 glider bomb was in fact a miniature aeroplane, with a wing span of 10 feet 2 inches. In the nose was fitted a 1,100 pound warhead, and after release the liquid fuel rocket motor under the fuselage accelerated the weapon to a speed of 370 m.p.h in 12 seconds. Then, the fuel exhausted, the motor cut and the missile coasted on in a shallow dive towards the target. The glider bomb's range depended upon the height at which it was released from the parent aircraft; the maximum was over eight miles if it was launched from 22,000 feet. At the rear of the weapon was a bright flare, to enable the bomb aimer in the parent aircraft to follow its progress in flight. The bomb aimer operated a small joy-stick controller, the movement of which fed the appropriate up-down-left-right impulses to a radio transmitter which in turn radiated them to the missile. Thus the bomb aimer had merely to steer the missile's tracking flare until it was

superimposed on the target, and hold it there until the weapon hit. Since the impact velocity was only about 450 m.p.h. the warhead had little penetrative capability, and the weapon was intended mainly for use against lightly armoured warships, and freighters in escorted convoys.

The second of the German anti-shipping weapons, the Ruhrstahl Fritz-X guided bomb*, was intended for use against heavily armoured targets. In appearance it resembled an ordinary bomb, except for the four stabilizing wings mounted mid-way along its body. Like the glider bomb, the Fritz-X was radio controlled by means of a joystick controller in the parent aircraft, and was tracked by means of a tail-mounted flare. The 3,100 pound bomb was unpowered; released from altitudes between 16,000 and 21,000 feet, it accelerated under the force of gravity to reach a speed close to that of sound.

The Fritz-X was aimed like a normal bomb using a bomb sight, and the bomb-aimer radioed correction signals only during the final part of the missile's trajectory. The problem of controlling such a weapon on to a target now deserves some consideration—it is

*Also known as the PC 1400 X and the X-1.*

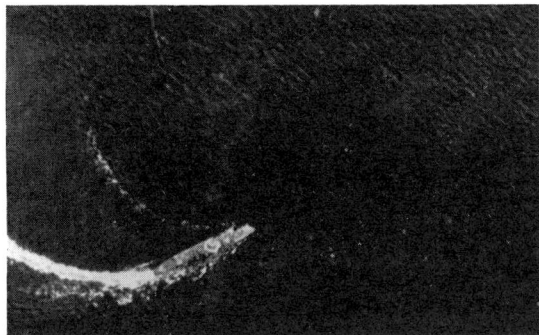

not as simple as it might at first appear. As anyone who has watched a falling bomb from an aircraft will testify, a correctly aimed bomb appears to be under-shooting until the last few seconds of its fall. Then it suddenly darts for the target. The reason for this is that while the bomb's forward speed is progressively reduced by the resistance of the air, that of the powered aircraft is not. As a result the bomber, flying at a steady speed over the ground, reaches a point some distance beyond the target when the bomb impacts. It is because he is looking backwards at the trajectory that the bomb-aimer gets the impression of an undershooting bomb.

The answer to the aiming problem was to somehow get the aircraft overhead the target at the moment of impact, so that by looking *down* the trajectory the bomb-aimer could feed the right correcting signals to the missile. The solution worked out by Max Kramer, the designer of the Fritz-X, was almost ingenious in its simplicity. After releasing the missile the pilot of the launching aircraft pulled his aircraft into a climb to 1,000 feet and lowered his flaps. In this way he rapidly reduced his speed from 210 m.p.h. to 120 m.p.h. and the aircraft arrived over the target at the same time as the bomb impacted.

*Three photographs taken from a remarkable series taken during the attack on the Italian battle fleet. Right to left, the flare of the second Fritz-X to hit the* Roma *can be seen closing in towards the desperately evading battleship. For clarity the flare has been indicated by a dotted line and a semi-circle. This bomb started a serious fire within the ship which reached the ammunition in the forward magazine . . . (see page 24) (via Bernhard Jope).*

In July 1943 two specialist units were formed to use the new guided missiles in action, the Second and Third *Gruppen* of K.G. 100. The former unit was equipped with the Do 217E, which had been modified to carry a maximum of two Hs 293's, one under each outer wing panel. The latter unit was equipped with the Do 217K-2, a high-flying version of the Do 217K with a wing span greater by 19 feet—a modification necessitated by the requirement for the Fritz-X bombs to be released from high level; two such bombs could be carried on the wings inboard of the engines, but as this load reduced the weight of fuel that could be carried and cut the range considerably, it was usual for only the starboard rack to be loaded before operational flights.

By August 1943 the missile-carrying units were trained and ready, and now they moved from their training airfields in Germany to operational bases in the south of France: II./K.G. 100 went to Cognac, III./K.G. 100 to Marseilles/Istres. The *Geschwader* commander was Major Bernhard Jope, who had earlier led a successful career flying anti-shipping strikes with the Focke Wulf Condor.*

*See Volume One.

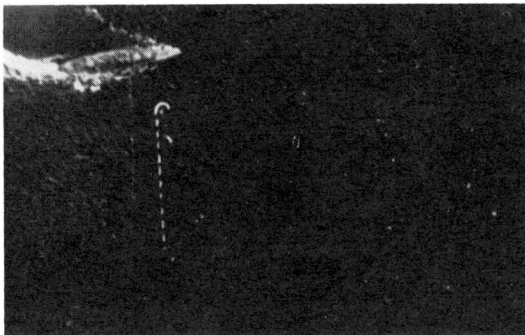
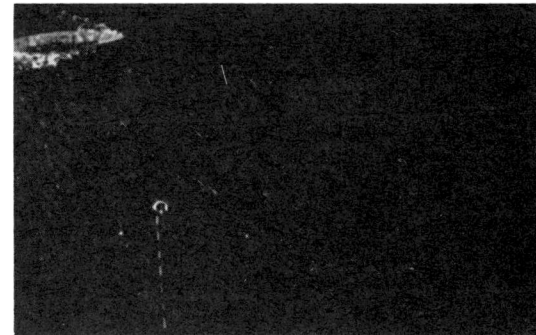

## IN ACTION WITH THE MISSILES

On the afternoon of August 25, 1943 12 Do 217's of Captain Molinus' II./K.G. 100 attacked a Royal Navy U-boat hunting group comprising seven ships, off the north-western tip of Spain. The attack was a failure: many of the glider bombs failed to function properly, and only superficial damage was caused to the corvettes. Nevertheless, since this was the first guided missile attack in history, a description of how it appeared to those on the receiving end may interest the reader.

The British ships were dispersed, and the Dorniers attacked them separately. It was at 1340 hours on the 25th that H.M.S. *Landguard's* lookout sighted three aircraft, reported as Ju 88's, six miles away on the starboard side and making towards the escort group.

*... and the ship blew up violently. Seconds later ... (Imp. War Mus.).*

The aircraft spent some time forming up and then, when they were off the starboard quarter at a range of about six miles, the sailors observed:

"A puff of smoke forming into a streamer appeared from the leading aircraft. At the time of firing the aircraft were on a reciprocal course to the ships, well out on the beam. The projectile was seen for some time apparently near the aircraft, but this was probably due to the fact that it was coming towards the ship at a constant bearing. Flashes were seen coming from the aircraft at about the time of the firing, but neither smoke nor flame from the projectile during the later stages of its run."

All in all this is a remarkably accurate description, considering the fact that the watchers had obviously never seen anything quite like this before. The missile came towards the ship "at a constant bearing" because it was flying along the line of sight between the aircraft and the ship; no smoke was seen coming from the missile during the later stages of the run because then the rocket motor had expended its fuel, and the bomb was gliding towards the target. The observers noted that:

"The projectile then banked exactly like an aircraft and set course towards the ship, descending

*... all that remained of the Italian ship was the bow and stern sections, which slowly sank beneath the waves (Imp. War Mus.).*

## ATTACK WITH FRITZ X GUIDED BOMB

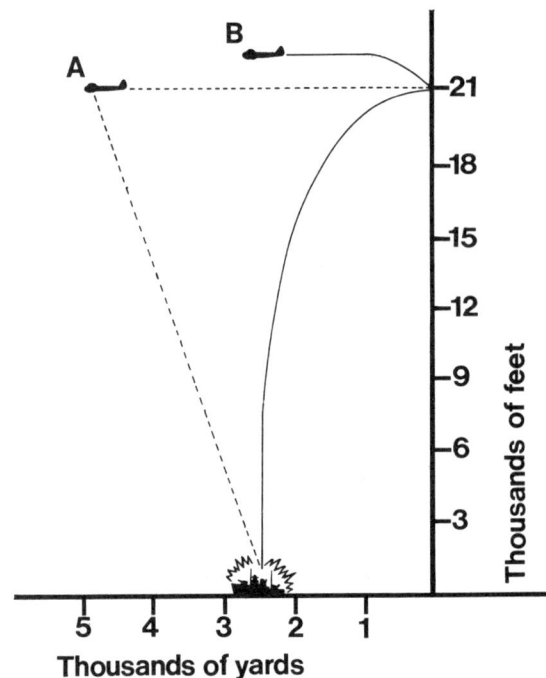

*Aircraft A flies over the target in the normal way after bomb release; it will be seen that an observer in this machine is unable to correct the missile in range. Aircraft B has climbed one thousand feet after bomb release, and thus has slowed down sufficiently to arrive over the target at the same time as the missile impacts; in this case the observer in the aircraft is able to control the missile for range during the final part of its trajectory.*

at an angle of about 15° or 20°. When about two cables* from the starboard quarter the bomb appeared to be pointing straight at the ship. Then it banked to starboard and lost height rapidly, falling in the sea one hundred yards off *Landguard's* starboard quarter and exploding on impact."

Three minutes later a second glider bomb was aimed at *Landguard* and curved in gradually towards the ship, cutting the log line about 130 feet from the stern. This bomb made no effort to turn towards the ship— obviously the radio control system had not functioned correctly. Five minutes later came yet another attack:

"*Landguard* altered course towards as the bomb was seen approaching. It actually crossed the bows from starboard to port and banked very rapidly in towards the ship, appearing to stall due to the steepness of its turn, and fell into the sea 40 yards away when pointing at the ship. The explosion threw up a column of water 60 feet high but did not shake the ship as much as a shallow depth charge. Several bits of projectile were thrown on board. Fire was opened on the projectile with an Oerlikon in the last stages of its flight."

The observer concluded:

"It was noticeable that the projectile approached the ship in the first and third attacks in a way that appeared to make a hit inevitable, but that in each case they lost power and dived into the sea short of the target."

Other ships in the escort group were also attacked but only H.M.S. *Bideford* suffered damage, and this was the result of a near miss.

During these attacks the Do 217's carried only one glider bomb, which was loaded on to the starboard wing rack. On the port side a drop-tank was carried, both to act as a counter-weight and to extend the range of the bomber; the tank was jettisoned at the same time as the glider bomb was released. Even if the distance to the target was not great, there were sound tactical reasons for loading each aircraft with only a single missile. In the first place, since only one glider bomb could be controlled from each aircraft at a time, two quite separate attacks would have been necessary if two missiles were carried and this would mean losing the advantage of the surprise factor. Moreover it would take some time for the launching aircraft to get into position again for the second attack, and during this period there would be a grave danger of enemy fighters arriving on the scene. In the second place, if

*About 400 yards.

the attack was successful and only one missile was needed the pilot would have to jettison the second missile, because it would have been an extremely dangerous undertaking to attempt to land the small Do 217 with a bomb under one of the outer wing panels and no counter-weight on the other side; it was undesirable to jettison the missile because they were very expensive, and at first were in short supply.

Two days after its initial missile attack, on August 27, II./K.G. 100 struck again and in the same place. This time the target was the five ship strong First

*Above: A Do 217K demonstrates its unusual retractable parachute speed brake. Some of the aircraft operating over Britain carried the device, which made possible rapid deceleration to shake off night fighters. When the parachute brake was no longer required a system of lines enabled the canopy to be collapsed, and the parachute was then retracted into its housing.*

*Below: A Dornier Do 217K of K.G. 2 taxies out at Eindhoven for a night operation.*

Support Group, and now the Hs 293 drew its first blood. The Canadian destroyer *Athabaskan* and the British corvette *Egret* both suffered hits, and the latter sank; another ship in the group, the corvette *Rother*, was damaged by near misses. Following this action the

Royal Navy withdrew its anti-submarine patrols from the Bay of Biscay, to positions outside the range of the missile-carrying Dorniers.

## THE ATTACK ON THE *ROMA*

Even as II./K.G. 100 was operating over the Bay of Biscay the Dorniers of its sister unit, III./K.G. 100, sat ready at their dispersal points around the airfield at Marseilles/Istres. Each aircraft carried an operational fuel load, and on the wing inboard of the starboard engine hung a single, light-blue coloured Fritz-X bomb. The reason for this continued high state of readiness was unknown to the rank and crewmen of the secret German unit; but clearly something big was in the wind. Rumours abounded. The favourite was that the Allies were about to invade the Italian mainland; if they did, the Fritz-X would come as a nasty shock to them ...

The only man at Istres to know the real reason for the alert was Major Bernhard Jope, *Geschwader* commander of K.G. 100. Jope had recently returned from Rome, where he had been given a top secret briefing on the military situation by the commander of the Second Air Force*, General Wolfram von Richtofen†. In the strictest confidence Jope was told of the latest disturbing development in the Mediterranean war: the Italians were on the point of concluding a separate peace with the Allies. And when they did their fleet was to sail to Malta and surrender, under the terms of the armistice‡.

So it came about that at the end of August 1943, while Germany and Italy *were still ostensibly fighting as allies,* Jope's aircraft were sitting ready and waiting to strike at the Italian fleet if it should move one inch outside its main base at La Spezia.

At 3 a.m. on the morning of September 9 the armistice came into effect and the Italian fleet sailed from La Spezia—three battleships, six cruisers and

eight destroyers. Almost immediately the news was flashed to the German headquarters in Rome, and from there to Jope in Istres.

Hastily III./K.G. 100 was brought to immediate readiness, and now the surprised crewmen learnt that they were about to go into action against their erstwhile ally. If the Italians were making for Malta they would certainly steer well clear of the German air bases in southern Italy, and probably pass to the west of Corsica; as the morning progressed the first reports from reconnaissance aircraft came in—the ships were indeed passing to the west of Corsica. There was a hasty briefing, and the aircrews received their final attack orders. By mid-day all was ready, and shortly after 2 p.m. 11 snub-nosed Dorniers took off from Istres and headed south-eastwards out to sea.

During their slow climb to altitude, the German aircraft flew in an untidy gaggle: since there was nothing to fear from enemy fighters in this part of the Mediterranean there was no call for a tight formation. It was a beautiful Mediterranean summer's day, and the visibility was almost unlimited. In the nose of each Dornier a crewman scanned the horizon through his binoculars. Just after 2.40 p.m. the Germans found what they were looking for: the tell-tale wakes of a number of large ships moving through the water at high speed.

The Dorniers ran in to bomb at levels around 20,000 feet, where the anti-aircraft fire was inaccurate and ineffective. As Jope recalls:

"From so high up we could not recognise the individual ships; we just picked upon the biggest we could see, and each ran in to bomb that."

Below the Dorniers, the Italian ships went into tight turns, twisting this way and that in an effort to put the Germans off their aim. In the face of normal high-level bombing such tactics would be successful: a bomb takes nearly three-quarters of a minute to fall from 20,000 feet, during which time a fast ship in open water could cover 700 yards forwards or to either side.

But Jope's aircraft were loaded with radio-controlled bombs, and now the manoeuvres afforded the ships little protection. After releasing the missile the German pilots pulled their aircraft up through 1,000 feet, then levelled out. Now the bomb aimer in the nose of each Dornier concentrated his entire attention on the missile's tracking flare, as he carefully steered it over the target and held it there. The first hit was on the Italian flagship, the battleship *Roma*. The bomb struck just to the starboard of the after mast, passed clean

through the ship and exploded immediately underneath it. Seriously damaged, the *Roma's* starboard steam turbines ground to a halt; the ship's speed fell to 16 knots. A few minutes later *Roma* was hit again, this time between the bridge and her "B" turret. Now the port steam turbines were also knocked out, and the battleship wallowed to a stop. Below decks a fierce fire raged, and *Roma* signalled that she was in "a desperate condition". A minute or so later, at 3.10 p.m., the flames reached her forward magazine and set off the ammunition stored there. There was a tremendous explosion and the ship folded up like a jack-knife; then she broke into two and sank, taking most of her crew with her.

Shortly after the attack on *Roma* her sister ship, the *Italia,* was hit on the bow by a Fritz-X; the battleship took on some 800 tons of water and her speed was reduced to 24 knots, but she was able to reach Malta unaided.

Jope and his men were denied the satisfaction of seeing the *Roma* break up, and they returned to Istres able to claim only that they had scored hits. To quote Jope again:

"We did not see the *Roma* explode. That happened after we left. We saw the explosions as the bombs hit, sure, but how often had we seen this before and then the ship managed to limp back to port?"

Only later, when the news was given out on the Allied news broadcasts, did the men of III./K.G. 100 learn how successful their attack had been.

On the same day as the Italian fleet set sail, the Allied forces did land on the mainland of Italy, at Salerno near Naples. Here again there was a large concentration of valuable shipping, just the sort of target for which the German guided weapons had been designed. Jope's men pressed home their attacks, and in the week that followed they scored hits on the battleship H.M.S. *Warspite*, and the cruisers H.M.S. *Uganda* and U.S.S. *Savanna,* causing severe damage to all three.

Some idea of the power of the Fritz-X may be gained from the damage suffered by *Warspite* when she was hit by a salvo of three of these weapons. One bomb scored a direct hit which penetrated six decks to explode on, and blow a hole through, the ship's double bottom; the other two bombs gashed the side compartments. One boiler room was demolished, and four of her other five were flooded. Fortunately there was no fire, for otherwise the consequences could well have been disastrous. As it was the ship lost all her steam,

---

*Luftflotte 2. The term "Air Force" is used here in the American sense, to denote a collection of flying units under a unified command, located within a set geographical area.*

†*Cousin of the First World War fighter ace.*

‡*German cryptographic experts had succeeded in de-cyphering certain top secret signals between London and Washington, including one relating to the fate of the Italian fleet once it was in Allied hands. Jope himself was not to learn the source of von Richtofen's information until 24 years had passed, when he was told of it by this author.*

she would not steer, and her radar and armament ceased to function. *Warspite* took on 5,000 tons of water, and her freeboard was lowered by five feet. Perhaps miraculously, in view of the scale of the damage, only nine men were killed and 14 were wounded. The battleship was towed back to Malta for temporary repairs, and did not see action again until June, 1944.

## MISSILE COUNTER-MEASURES

The months of August and September, 1943, marked the high-water mark in the fortunes of the *Kampfgeschwader* 100 missile-carrying Dorniers. The attacks had indeed come as a nasty surprise to the Allies, and Mr. Churchill rebuked his scientific advisor, Lord Cherwell, for not having provided him with any warning. On the September 20 Lord Cherwell replied:

"Even the most unceasing vigilance and the most intensive study cannot ensure that we should foresee all the inventions or developments that he (the enemy) may have made. But if and when such novel weapons are used a remedy will no doubt be forthcoming. An interval of course there may be before we have it, but nothing will be left undone to shorten the gap. More than this of course we cannot promise."

The best way to counter the German guided weapons was to prevent the Dorniers from reaching the shipping, for the effectiveness of an air-launched weapon is not one ounce better than the ability of the parent aircraft to get it to within launching range of the target. Accordingly the next landing, at Anzio in January, 1944, enjoyed lavish fighter protection and the missile-carrying aircraft suffered heavily. In spite of double the Salerno effort, with attacks by Do 217's of K.G. 100 and the He 177's of K.G. 40, the only major German success was the sinking of the cruiser H.M.S. *Spartan*.

By the early part of 1944 the Allies had taken the technical, as well as the operational, measure of the German guided missiles. The radio control system fitted to the weapons was a simple one, and easily jammed. Two types of radio countermeasures transmitter were employed. One simply blotted out the parent aircraft's transmissions altogether; the other, more subtly, radiated a full up, down, left or right signal on the German control frequency—to swing the missile hard off course.

On June 6, 1944, the long-awaited Allied invasion of France took place. The strength of the day and night fighter cover at the bridgehead exceeded anything yet encountered by the *Luftwaffe*, and the anti-shipping and bombing aircraft smashed themselves bravely but ineffectively against this impenetrable barrier. The headquarters ship *Bulolo* suffered bomb damage on June 7, the frigate H.M.S. *Lawford* was sunk on June 8, and on the night of June 12 the destroyer H.M.S. *Boadicea* was hit and sunk by air-launched torpedoes off Portland; in addition to these naval losses, one landing craft and two merchant ships were sunk by air attack during the first ten days of the invasion. Thus, of the many hundreds of ships at sea during this period, only five were lost to direct air attack. On the rare occasions when the German bombers did get through the defences to launch their missiles, the ships' own radio jamming transmitters successfully neutralized the weapons.

In the end the Germans abandoned the idea of direct attacks against the ships, and instead devoted their efforts to mining the narrow seas. In the following six weeks more than 3,000 mines of various types were sown, including many of the new pressure mines which could be countered only by restricting all movement to a snail's pace while in shallow water. By the end of the month the mining campaign had caused the loss of seven destroyers, two minesweepers, 16 auxiliary vessels and merchantmen ". . . and the Trinity House vessel *Alert*." The mines caused considerable inconvenience, but such losses were not going to turn away the greatest invasion armada ever assembled.

Following the collapse of the German aviation fuel production in the summer of 1944, several bomber *Geschwader* were disbanded, including K.G. 2 and K.G. 100 which at that time operated the overwhelming majority of the Do 217 bombers. As a result the type saw very little action during the remainder of the war, though a few of them were used, unsuccessfully, in April, 1945, to launch glider bombs against the Russian crossings over the Oder River.

The Dornier Do 217 was a fast modern design, well liked by the crews who flew it. But it did not achieve greatness because it entered service at a time when the defences in the west and in the Mediterranean were able to inflict heavy losses whenever sustained operations were attempted. Only once, when it was used as a missile-launcher during the summer of 1943, did the Do 217 look like becoming a real menace to the Allies. But the menace was soon contained, and the world's first guided missiles had little opportunity after that to demonstrate their prowess.

## SPECIFICATION Do 217E

**Crew**
Four.

**Power Plant**
Two 1,580 h.p. BMW 801 14-cylinder air-cooled radials.

**Dimensions**
Span: 62 ft. 4 in.; Length: 59 ft. 8½ in.; Wing area: 614 sq. ft.

**Weights**
Empty 19,533 lb. Loaded 33,070 lb.

**Armament**
Varied, but typically one 13 mm. gun fixed firing forwards, another in the dorsal turret and a third firing downwards and rearwards from the rear of the cockpit; two 7·9 mm. machine-guns firing sideways from the cockpit sides.

**Maximum bomb load**
8,800 lb. or two Hs 293 glider bombs.

**Maximum speed**
320 m.p.h.

**Maximum range**
1,430 miles (normal fuel); 1,740 miles (with auxiliary fuel).

**Service ceiling**
24,000 ft.

# Heinkel He 177 Griffon

THE Heinkel He 177 Griffon* was to have been the *Luftwaffe* equivalent of Lancasters and Halifaxes, the Fortresses and Liberators: a long-range hard-hitting bomber able to penetrate deeply into an enemy's territory to strike at his vitals. Such were the hopes that were never to be realized.

If historians are agreed on one thing regarding the He 177, it is that this aircraft had no effect at all on the course of the Second World War. Well over a thousand of these bombers were built, but it is doubtful whether more than 200 of them were ever used on operations. During the latter part of the war Allied reconnaissance aircraft often returned with photographs of parks in Germany full of He 177's; analysis would later reveal that "Absence of track activity suggests that these machines are not being worked on." When the war

*Grief

ended the 900 or so He 177's remaining, most of them in mint condition, found their way into scrapyards all over Europe. It was an ignominious ending not only to the saga of the He 177, but also to the idea of a German strategic bomber force to rival those of Great Britain and the U.S.A.

It was early in 1938 that the German Air Ministry passed details of its heavy bomber requirement to the Heinkel company. This specification called for an

*An extremely rare photograph of Heinkel He 177's carrying Hs 293 glider bombs, one under each wing. The airfield is Bordeaux/Merignac—note the bomb damage to the hangars resulting from Allied attacks—and the aircraft belong to the anti-shipping unit II./K.G. 40. For a long time the most important bomber in the planned Luftwaffe re-equipment programme, the He 177 arrived in front line service in quantity eighteen months late, in the autumn of 1943; and even then it was still far from perfect (Franz Selinger).*

aircraft with a maximum speed of 335 m.p.h., able to carry 4,400 lb. of bombs out to a radius of 1,000 miles or alternatively 2,200 lb. out to 1,800 miles. All in all this was a formidable specification, calling as it did for an aircraft able to outrun any fighter, and outperform by a considerable margin any bomber then in service. To meet it, Siegfried Guenther, Heinkel's chief designer, was forced to resort to a number of untried features.

Guenther would have like to have used two 2,000 h.p. engines to power his new bomber. But in 1938 the Germans possessed no motor capable of 2,000 h.p., and indeed they had not one in large scale service by 1945. In an effort to get the power of four 1,000 h.p. engines for the drag penalty of a twin-engine installation, Guenther decided to use two paired Daimler Benz DB 601 motors; in this coupled installations, known as the DB 606, the two DB 601's were con-

nected to drive a single airscrew by means of a clutch arrangement. This double engine, two of which were to power the He 177, developed 2,600 h.p. for take-off.

To reduce drag still further, Guenther plumped for the revolutionary evaporative-cooling method. The DB 601 ran very hot, and was built to do so. In the proposed arrangement the coolant liquid—water with an anti-freeze additive—was pressurized. Thus it was possible to heat the water to 110°C before steam formed in the engine. The super-heated water was then ducted away and depressurized, at which point steam did form. Then the water was separated off and returned to the motor, while the steam was condensed by feeding it through pipes in the wing cooled by the airflow. After condensation the water formed from the steam was also fed back into the engine. Since it did away with the need for the drag-producing external radiators, the system promised to make possible an extremely clean aerodynamic layout. Flight tests showed that the method worked quite well on the small experimental He 100 single seat fighter; but it soon became clear that evaporative cooling would not dissipate sufficient heat if fitted to the He 177, and the idea was dropped before the first prototype flew.

The decision to install conventional radiators started a vicious circle, for the resultant extra drag meant that the bomber would fly slower for the same power setting. Thus more fuel was used in covering a given distance, and more had to be carried if the bomber was to meet its range specification. Additional tanks had to be fitted into the wings, and the wings had to be strengthened to take the extra weight, with the result that the all-up weight rose and the speed fell still further.

The next problem came when the *Luftwaffe* decided that it wanted the He 177 to be able to dive-bomb. Certainly there were great advantages to be gained in accuracy, if it could. However the dive bombing manoeuvre, and especially the pull-out afterwards, placed a great strain on the airframe. As a result the aircraft's structure had to be strengthened, which gave a further twist to the weight-drag-speed-range-more weight spiral.

The He 177 made its first flight on November 19, 1939, piloted by the head of Rechlin's flight test section, Dipl. Ing Francke. After only 12 minutes airborne Francke was forced to bring the aircraft back to Rostock/Marienehe, when the engines began to show signs of overheating; he also complained of a certain lack of stability, and a tendency to elevator flutter.

The second prototype flew shortly after the first, and was generally similar. Another Rechlin pilot, Rickert, used this machine for the diving trials; during the first test dive it developed a severe control flutter and the aircraft broke up in the air. Following this incident the first, third, fourth and fifth prototypes of the new bomber were given larger tail surfaces.

When the diving trials were resumed the fourth prototype failed to pull out of a dive and crashed into the Baltic; the cause was put down to a malfunction of the airscrew pitch mechanism. Soon afterwards, early in 1941, the fifth prototype suffered an engine fire while airborne and crashed.

Thus three out of the first five prototypes of the He 177 had crashed during testing. The control flutter problem was soon cured, but that of the engine fires was to dog the bomber for most of its life. The causes were many and varied. Initially the lubrication to the engines was poor, with the result that the connecting rod bearings would seize to cause the rods to smash through the crank case and spill oil over the red-hot exhaust manifolds. Moreover, if the throttles were handled roughly the fuel injectors would leak and allow neat fuel to run down into the bottom of the engine bay; if the aircraft was flying at a high angle of attack, for example if it was landing or flying at high altitude, the fuel would run to the rear of the compartment and drip on to the hot engine exhausts.

The fourth prototype He 177, landing after an early test flight. This aircraft crashed into the sea following the failure of the propeller pitch control mechanism (Franz Selinger).

There were other problems. As the flight testing progressed it became clear that, requirement or not, the He 177 was too big and stable to make a dive bomber. Whilst the machine was remarkably handy for a long range bomber, it just was not manoeuvrable enough to make diving attacks. To get the He 177 to dive at all it was necessary to cut the speed right back before one could get the nose down. Having established the aircraft in the dive the engines could be opened up again, but acceleration was slow, and before a sufficiently high speed had built up it was time to pull out of the dive. And even with its specially strengthened airframe, the He 177 proved unequal to the stresses imposed upon it during the pull out of the dive. As an admission of the bomber's unsuitability for the role, the dive brakes were left off all aircraft built after the pre-production batch.

Following the pre-production batch of 35 aircraft, used exclusively for trials purposes, came 130 production He 177A-1's. The latter were completed between March, 1942 and June, 1943, but there was ample evidence that the He 177 was still a long way from being suitable for service use; in the event all 130 of the He 177A-1's were relegated to second line duties, even after 34 had been delivered to I./K.G. 40 at Bordeaux/Merignac in the summer of 1942 in a premature attempt to introduce the type into large scale service.

The second production version of the bomber, the He 177A-3, featured an increased armament, a five-foot fuselage extension aft of the wing to improve stability and eight-inch longer engine nacelles redesigned to cut out many of the known causes of fires. The first examples of this sub-type were delivered to Bomber Replacement-Training *Geschwader* 50* late in 1942. Crews and aircraft from the unit were hastily formed into Long-range Bomber *Gruppe* 2†, which was rushed to Russia to fly supplies to the German troops cut off at Stalingrad. But mid-Russia in winter time, with only makeshift servicing arrangements, was no

*Ergaenzungs Kampfgeschwader 50.
†Fernkampfgruppe 2.

He 177A-3 belonging to Pilot School (B) 16, at Burg airfield near Magdeburg (R. C. Seeley).

Heinkel He 177A-5 of the First Gruppe of Kampfgeschwader 100. This aircraft, operating from Rheine in Germany and Chateaudun in France, took part in the night attacks on Great Britain during the spring of 1944.

*The remaining views will be found overleaf.*

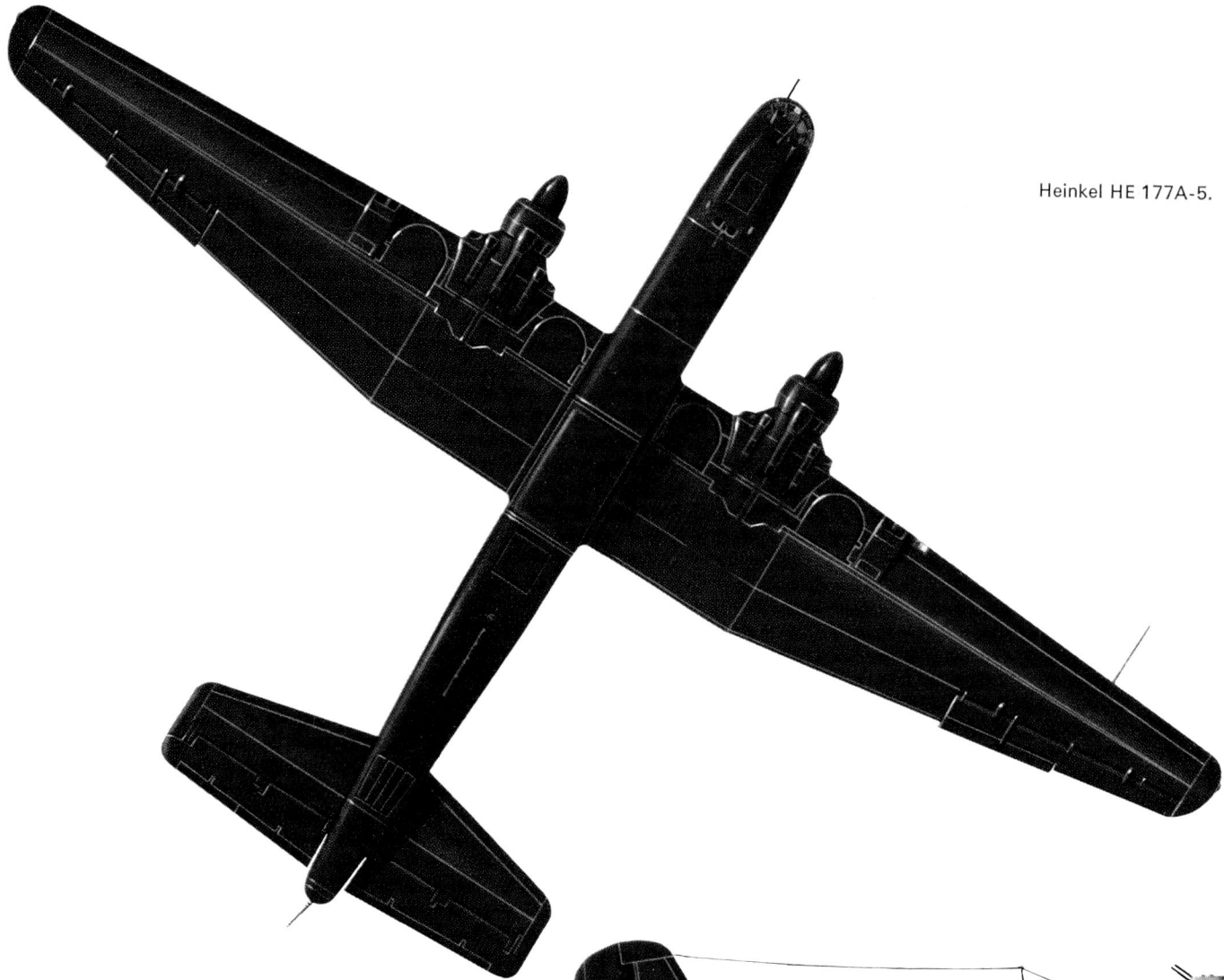

Heinkel HE 177A-5.

*Several He 177's were lost following fires in the Daimler Benz DB 610 coupled inverted "V" motors. These fires gave trouble throughout the whole of the engine's service life . . . (Imp. War Mus.).*

place for the complicated and largely untried He 177. Of the 40 or so examples sent to Saporoschje only seven were serviceable for the first lift into the city; Major Scheede led this first operation, but his Heinkel crashed and he was killed. Following this poor start the He 177's—which had in any case proved to be inefficient transport aircraft because there was little room for stowing supplies—reverted to the bomber role but with no greater success. The old problem of engine fires had still not been solved completely, and seven aircraft were lost to this cause alone with no action on the part of the Russians. As soon as the Stalingrad pocket fell, in February, 1943, the surviving He 177's were flown back to Germany.

One hundred and seventy He 177-A3's were built before production shifted to the A-5. This sub-type was fitted with two DB 610 motors, which developed a maximum of 3,100 h.p.; but like the earlier DB 606 this was a coupled engine, and many of the old problems remained. However the *Luftwaffe* desperately needed a long-range bomber, and the He 177A-5 was ordered into large scale production. By the end of 1943 a total of 261 examples of this sub-type had issued from the Heinkel factory at Oranienburg and the Arado factory at Warnemuende. That the bomber still had its faults was acknowledged, but the German Air Ministry judged it suitable for issue in quantity to front-line units.

## ANTI-SHIPPING OPERATIONS

From the beginning of the war *Kampfgeschwader* 40 had been earmarked to receive the He 177 to replace its frail Fw 200's*. Now, in the summer of 1943,

*See Volume One.

. . . *often with spectacular results (Horst von Riesen).*

aircraft and trained anti-shipping crews began to arrive at the unit's operational airfields in France. These machines were equipped to carry either Hs 293 glider bombs, Fritz-X guided bombs or torpedoes on the outer wing external racks.

The He 177 first went into action in the anti-shipping role on the afternoon of November 21, 1943. Major Mons led 20 glider bomb carrying He 177's of II./K.G. 40 against the 73 ship strong convoy SL 139/MKS 30† when it was at a position 420 miles north east of Cape Finistere. The Germans concentrated their attentions on the merchant ships *Marsa* and *Delius*, which were straggling a little way behind the main formation, and sank the former and damaged the latter. They also launched glider bombs at two frigates, *Calder* and *Drury* of the First Escort Group, without success; the ships evaded the bombs by a

†*SL—Sierra Leone to Britain; MKS—North Africa to Britain.*

combination of high speed manoeuvring, firing at the missiles themselves, and letting off Very flares to confuse the glider bomb controllers. Three He 177's did not return from this attack.

Five days later, at dusk on the 26th, II./K.G. 40 struck again. This time Mons led 14 He 177's against convoy KMF 26 as it passed Cape Bougie on the Algerian coast. The unit pressed home its attack with great élan, undeterred by the convoy's strong defences, and scored glider bomb hits on the liner *Rohna*, which sank. The darkness and the heavy swell impeded rescue work, and more than a thousand American soldiers—more than half those embarked—lost their lives. But on the German side the losses were proportional to the success achieved: four of the bombers were shot down, and three more crashed on landing back at Bordeaux/Merignac. Mons himself was killed during this operation, which with the earlier one had cost II./K.G. 40 nearly half its strength.

After this K.G. 40 restricted itself to the less effective

but also less costly night attacks, and kept up a steady pressure on Allied convoys passing through the Mediterranean. The He 177's still attacked with glider bombs, their attacks being synchronized with those of torpedo-carrying Ju 88's and flare-dropping aircraft.

The lull ended on January 22, 1944, when Allied forces landed at Anzio, just to the south of Rome. The He 177's of II./K.G. 40 operated alongside the missile-carrying Do 217's of K.G. 100, and suffered accordingly. Following a few weeks intensive operations against the Anzio bridgehead, II./K.G. 40 resumed its harassing operations against the Mediterranean convoys.

## OPERATION STEINBOCK

During Operation *Steinbock*, the renewed German night attack upon London, the He 177 operated for the first time against the British capital. Two *Gruppen* of them, I./K.G. 40 and I./K.G. 100, with a total of 46 aircraft operated together from the airfields at Rheine and Chateaudun.

During the very first of the new attacks, on the night of January 21, 1944, Flying Officer H. Kemp of No. 151 Squadron "bagged" the first He 177 to be shot down over the United Kingdom. Kemp was flying his Mosquito to investigate a searchlight cone when his radar operator, Flight Sergeant J. Maidment, observed a contact on the radar dead ahead at a range of two miles. Kemp closed in and caught sight of his quarry, but was himself seen and the bomber went into a violent evasive manoeuvre. The Mosquito crewmen lost contact, but were able to regain it soon afterwards. Kemp closed in and opened up with his four 20 mm. cannon; he saw hits on the port wing then a large explosion, in the light of which he could make out the large swastika on the tail of the bomber. The target, an He 177 of I./K.G. 40, went into a steep dive and crashed near Haslemere in Surrey.

Typical of the *Steinbock* attacks was that on London on April 18. The target was the city itself, and a total of 125 bombers of all types set out. Amongst those taking part were five He 177's of Captain von Kalkreuth's I./K.G. 100. After taking off from Rheine, near Muenster, the crews climbed as high as they possibly could while over friendly territory. For the

*A rare formation shot of He 177's, almost certainly machines of the anti-shipping unit II./K.G. 40 (R. C. Seeley).*

actual penetration of the defences they flew in a shallow dive at high speed, tactics which made it difficult for even the superlative Mosquitoes to intercept effectively. After releasing their bombs the crews withdrew at low level. But in spite of these unorthodox methods one of the He 177's, piloted by Warrant Officer Heinz Reis, failed to return.

Potentially the He 177's represented a formidable element in Peltz's attacking force, but this potential was not realized. As Peltz now recalls:

"It was true that the He 177 carried the greatest bomb load of any of the types under my command, but technically she was very complicated. Because of this the proportion of aircraft available for any attack was low in comparison with the other types."

## BOMBER DESTROYER

An interesting idea mooted in the summer of 1944 was the use of He 177's with air-to-air rocket armaments to counter the powerful American Fortress and Liberator formations. Five of the He 177's were

*This He 177 of I./K.G. 100 took part in Operation* Steinbock, *the night bombing attacks on Great Britain in the early part of 1944. Note the lack of fuselage crosses on this machine ( R. C. Seeley).*

attached to Major Christl's Test Flight 25*, based at Finow. The He 177's were fitted with a battery of 33 upwards-firing rockets, mounted in three rows of 11 in the upper fuselage. The rockets were inclined forwards at an angle of 30 degrees to the vertical, and inclined slightly to starboard. For fire control purposes the battery was divided into two groups, one of 18 and one of 15. The pilot could select to fire the rockets all at once, or those in either of the two groups, or else singly. The missiles were sighted by means of a reflector sight fitted to the window above the pilot's head.

The rockets were harmonized to converge on a point 6,000 feet above, and slightly in front and to starboard of, the firing aircraft. Thus the latter could attack while itself remaining clear of the defensive fire from the bomber formation. However this novel arrangement promised no such immunity from the American long-range escort fighters, and the idea was dropped.

## OPERATIONS ON THE EASTERN FRONT

The He 177 units in France operated alongside the Do 217's of K.G. 2 and III./K.G. 100 during the

*Erprobungs Kommando 25.

*Close-up of the aerials of the* Hohentwiel *ship-search radar, seen on the nose of an He 177 of II./K.G. 40 (Franz Selinger).*

He 177A-5 of III./K.G. 1, which operated with the type on the Eastern Front in the summer of 1944 (Horst von Riesen).

attempt to beat off the Allied invasion of France, but as we have seen they were able to achieve little. But the failure of the anti-invasion attacks did not see the end of the He 177's operational career for now, at last, the much-maligned bomber was to prove itself.

Even as the He 177's of I./K.G. 40 and I./K.G. 100 were striking at the British capital, a full *Geschwader* was converting to the heavy bomber in Germany. The unit was *Kampfgeschwader* 1, commanded by Lieutenant Colonel Horst von Riesen. In May the first *Gruppe* was ready for action, and under the greatest secrecy the unit moved out to its operational airfields in East Prussia; the bases were in the Koenigsberg area, centred on Prowehren and Seerappen. Before the end of the month the second and third *Gruppen* arrived and von Riesen's *Geschwader*, comprising as it did some 90 He 177's, represented the most powerful strategic striking force possessed by either side on the Eastern Front.

The He 177's of K.G. 1 went into action as soon as they arrived in East Prussia, striking at Russian supply centres and troop assembly areas. Strategic targets were within the range of the heavy bombers, but K.G. 1 made no attempt to hit them: the expected Russian summer offensive could not now be long delayed, and the German soldiers needed all the help they could possibly get.

During these attacks, usually carried out from high level in daylight, losses were extremely low. The Russian Air Force, equipped mainly for the low level interception and ground attack roles, could do little to hinder the high-flying bombers. Those fighters which did claw themselves up to 20,000 feet to the He 177's attack level showed the greatest respect for the defensive armament of the bombers and attacks were rarely pressed home.

Over Russia K.G. 1 made several pattern-bombing attacks. In the most powerful of these von Riesen himself led a formation of 87 He 177's against the important railway centre at Velikye Luki, 300 miles to the west of Moscow. The force must have made an impressive sight, as it attacked in a formation of three

HE 177 of K.G.1, showing the night camouflage worn by some of this unit's aircraft. (Horst von Riesen).

*The Germans carried out a number of interesting experiments with towed fuel tanks fitted with auxiliary lifting aerofoils. In this case the towing aircraft is an He 177.*

closely spaced "V" shaped waves, each wave comprising a *Gruppe* of some 30 He 177's; unfortunately no photographs of these massed attacks seem to have survived. Prior to the pattern-bombing attack the spacing of individual aircraft in the waves, and the interval between the waves, had been carefully calculated to give the required bomb density at the target. In the lead aircraft von Riesen traversed the centre of the target and as his bomb aimer saw the far side of the objective slide under his bomb sight von Riesen broadcast the bomb-release signal to his *Geschwader*.

During these intensive operations von Riesen's unit experienced little trouble with overheating engines. By the summer of 1944 the various modifications had greatly reduced the fire risk. Moreover the root cause of the fires—over-rough use of the throttles when running the engines up to full power, and holding this setting for too long—was well known. All von Riesen's pilots had been warned of the danger and instructed in avoiding it, and when engine fires did occur in K.G. 1 they were generally the result of engine mis-handling by inexperienced pilots.

On June 23, 1944, the Russians launched their long-awaited offensive, on the central front. The powerful onslaught smashed through the German lines, and in places the defeat became a rout. The Italian and southern fronts were combed for ground attack aircraft to help stem the flood; but all was in vain as the Russian tanks continued to roll westwards. In desperation Goering personally telephoned von Riesen and ordered him to send his *Geschwader* into action against the advancing tanks. It was a reckless way to use a big aircraft like the He 177, for to hit such a small

*Close-up of the rear gun turret of the He 177A-5.*

fast moving target the bombers would have to attack at very low altitudes. But when von Riesen raised a questioning voice Goering would not listen, and insisted that the operation be mounted. In an attempt to make the best of a bad job von Riesen sent out his He 177's after the tanks in pairs, in the hope that the combined fire-power from such a pair would provide a greater degree of protection from the fighters. But in spite of this the operation was a fiasco. The *Geschwader* lost nearly a quarter of the 40 or so He 177's committed, mainly to low-flying Russian fighters; it is doubtful whether any tanks were destroyed. The

dangerous low-level tactics were not repeated, and K.G. 1 resumed its high level pattern bombing attacks.

On July 20, K.G. 1 operated with almost its entire strength, the individual *Gruppen* attacking separate targets from high level. As is usual when aircraft form up into a large formation, the He 177's of K.G. 1 orbited a prominent geographical feature—in this case one of the distinctive Masury lakes in East Prussia. Just to the west of the lakes was a heavily wooded area over which the crews were specifically ordered not to fly: this was Rastenburg, Hitler's war headquarters. What happened that day is best told by von Riesen himself:

"At mid-day we assembled over one corner of the lake to the east of the Rastenburg prohibited area. To assemble 80 aircraft into three formations takes a lot of time, and as luck would have it a couple of the aircraft developed engine fires. My crews had been previously briefed that in this event they were to release their bombs "safe" (i.e. set so that they did not go off when they hit the surface) and aimed into the lake. This the crews did, and I set off eastwards with one of my *Gruppen* to make the attack.

"It was about five o'clock in the afternoon when I landed back at Prowehren, and I did not get to my headquarters until six o'clock. There I was met by my adjutant, who looked very serious. He ushered me into an empty office and said 'A terrible thing has happened. One of our machines obviously did not drop its bombs "safe"; moreover they landed on the Fuehrer's headquarters and caused an explosion there.' I nearly fainted. I thought that if it was true I would obviously be held responsible, and that would be the end. Then we heard a special bulletin on the radio: a news-flash stated that there had been an explosion at Hitler's headquarters, but did not go into detail.

"I tried to get in touch with the two crews who had dropped the bombs into the lake. But one had made a forced landing many miles away and could not be contacted, and the other had had to bale out and nobody had any idea where they were.

"Then I telephoned the Corps headquarters, and was told yes, something had happened. They were sending a legal officer to collect evidence for a possible court martial—mine."

There followed a very worrying couple of hours of interviews, before von Riesen's Corps commander telephoned and told him that he was "off the hook". The explosion had in fact been a deliberate attempt on Hitler's life, but von Riesen was in no way responsible. This was the famous July 20th Bomb Plot.

Heinkel He 177A-5 flown by Lieutenant Colonel Horst von Riesen, commander of Kampfgeschwader 1. This aircraft operated on the Eastern Front during the summer of 1944, from bases centred on Prowehren and Seerappen in East Prussia.

*The remaining views will be found overleaf.*

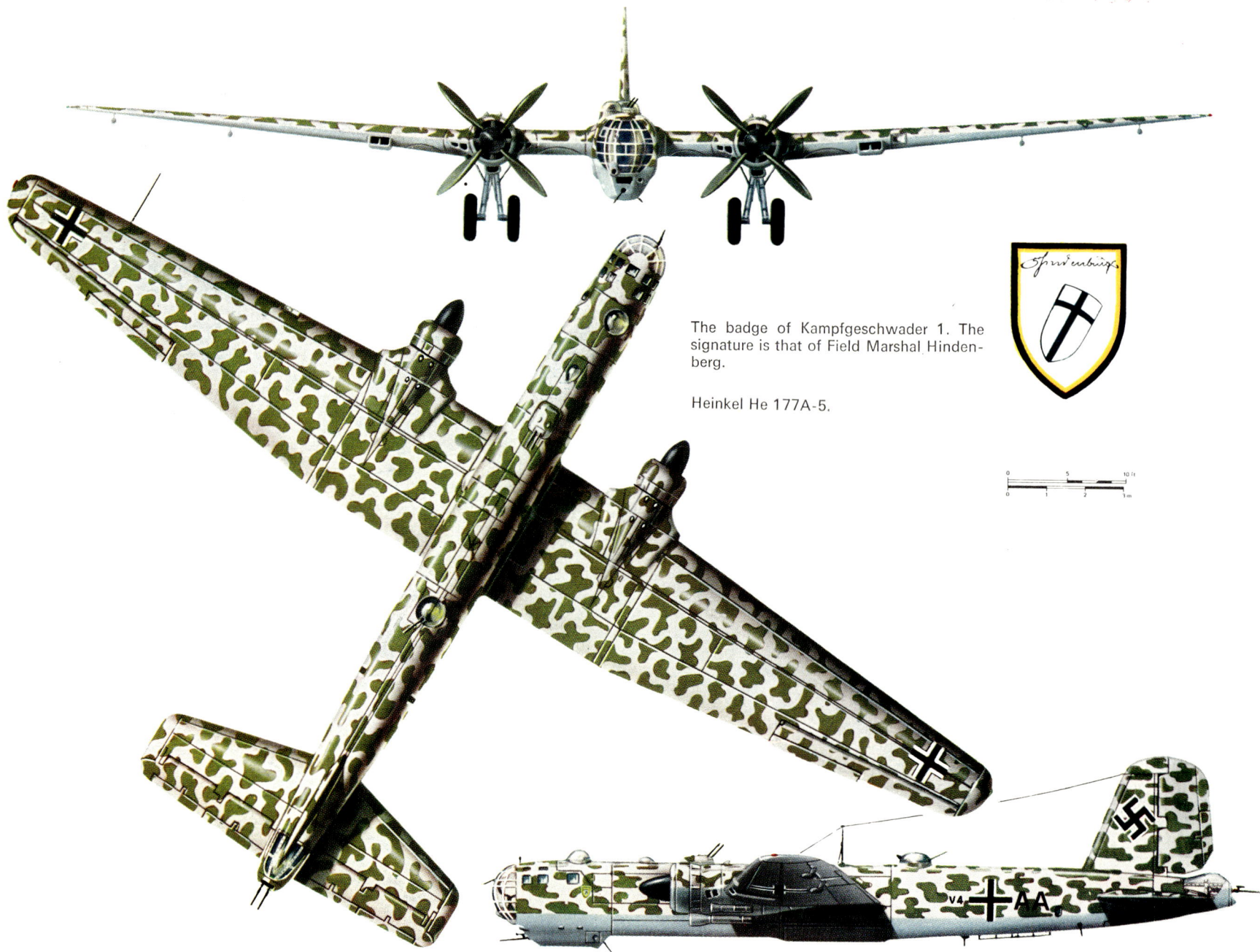

The badge of Kampfgeschwader 1. The signature is that of Field Marshal Hinden-berg.

Heinkel He 177A-5.

Junkers Ju 188A of the Second Gruppe of Kampfgeschwader 2, which operated from Vannes, France, during the night attacks on Britain during the spring of 1944. This aircraft was piloted by Sergeant Hans Engelke, with Leading Aircraftman Rudi Prasse as the bomb aimer/navigator.

*The remaining views will be found overleaf.*

Junkers Ju 188A.

*Lieutenant Colonel Horst von Riesen commanded K.G. 1 in the summer of 1944. Operating on the Eastern Front, this unit was the only* Geschwader *to be fully equipped with the He 177.*

imposed serious limitations on von Riesen's force: on one occasion enemy fighter-bombers caught the vital train, and not a drop of fuel arrived; as a result the operations planned for the following day had to be cancelled. In the spring of 1944 the British and American strategic air forces made a series of devastating attacks on German fuel producing centres. The production of high octane aviation petrol fell from 195,000 tons in May, 1944 to 52,000 tons in June, 35,000 tons in July and a paltry 16,000 tons in August. For an 80 aircraft attack K.G. 1 required 480 tons of fuel, which equalled an average day's output from the entire German industry in August, 1944.

There could be no arguing with the simple arithmetic: there just was no fuel to keep the heavy bombers going. Only fighter operations in air defence were allowed to continue unrestricted; even reconnaissance flights were limited, and fighter-bomber support was to be given to the army only in "decisive situations". The men of K.G. 1 were ordered to fly their aircraft back to Germany, where this and many other famous bomber units were disbanded. Thus fate dealt its final and most cruel blow to the He 177, at the very moment when it was achieving the success which had eluded it for so long. At the same time production of all bombers—except the jet propelled types—was cut back in favour of the Emergency Fighter Programme. The heavy piston engined bombers were wheeled in to the aircraft parks, where they collected rust and birds' nests until the end came and they were scrapped. Their demise marked the virtual end of the *Luftwaffe* as an offensive striking arm.

## THE FUEL FAMINE

Within a few days of the Rastenburg explosion K.G. 1 ceased operations, at a time when the German soldiers were crying out for all the help they could get. It was nothing to do with the Russian air defences, which had been a negligible factor so long as the bombers remained at high level, nor was it due to any shortcomings on the part of the He 177. The cause was far more serious, and was to have far-reaching effects on the German conduct of the war from then on: the crippling shortage of fuel, which was now bringing about a creeping paralysis within the German armed forces.

Each He 177 required about six tons of fuel for a medium range operation. Supplies had always been tenuous so far as K.G. 1 was concerned. There was no reserve of fuel at the airfields, and as the specially allocated fuel trains arrived the bombers were refuelled and sent into action. This hand-to-mouth existence

## SPECIFICATION HE 177 A-5

**Crew**
Six.

**Power plant**
Two 2,950 h.p Daimler Benz DB 610 24-cylinder liquid cooled engines

**Dimensions**
Span: 103 ft. 1¾ in. Length 66 ft. 11¼ in. Wing area: 1,098 sq. ft.

**Weight**
Empty: 37,038 lb. Maximum loaded: 68,343 lb.

**Armament**
Varied, but typically one 20 mm. cannon firing forwards from the lower part of the nose, a pair of 7·9 mm. guns firing forwards from the upper part of the nose, a pair of 7·9 mm. guns firing rearwards from the nose gondola, a pair of 13 mm. guns in the remotely controlled dorsal barbette, a single 13 mm. gun in the manually operated rear dorsal turret. and a single 20 mm. cannon in the rear gun position.

**Maximum bomb load**
13,200 lb. carried internally and externally.

**Maximum speed**
303 m.p.h.

**Maximum range**
3,400 miles carrying two Hs 293 missiles.

**Service ceiling**
26,250 ft.

# Junkers Ju 188

THE Junkers Ju 188 was a progressive development of the highly successful Ju 88 bomber*. With a wing span 6 feet 7 inches longer, and two engines each developing some 500 h.p. more, the Ju 188 was a much better high altitude bomber than the Ju 88A; it was faster and more manoeuvrable at height, and was more pleasant to handle. But the Ju 188 was only a little better than the improved Ju 88, the "S" sub-type, and it never did completely replace its predecessor in the front-line bomber units. By the beginning of 1944 production of the bomber version of the Ju 188 had ceased, after 446 examples had been built†. While this bomber never did form a major part of the striking force of the *Luftwaffe* it did operate over England on many occasions between the summer of 1943 and the summer of 1944, and so is of special interest to the British reader.

The Ju 188 was essentially a re-worked Ju 88 with longer, pointed wings for better high altitude performance, and more powerful BMW 801 motors. The fully

*Described in Volume One.*

*† A further 570 reconnaissance versions were built, 465 of them in 1944 and 1945 after production of the bomber version had ended.*

glazed nose section—a feature of the unsuccessful Ju 88B—was adopted, together with enlarged tail surfaces to improve stability. The first prototype of the Ju 188 flew early in 1942. Development work proceeded at a low priority until the autumn of that year, when the *Luftwaffe* ordered the type into production. In February, 1943, the first production Ju 188's left the Junkers factory at Bernburg near Dessau.

The German Air Ministry had intended that two sub-types of the Ju 188 should be produced simultaneously, the "A" powered by the 1,776 h.p. Jumo 213, and the otherwise identical "E" powered by the 1,600 h.p. BMW 801. This move was intended to allow for possible shortages of either type of engine, and on this occasion it paid off. Quantity production of the Jumo 213 was slow getting into its stride, and in the event the first aircraft produced were for the most part

*Junkers Ju 188E of the Pathfinder unit I./K.G. 66, flown by Second Lieutenant Hans Altrogge over Britain during 1943 and 1944. This aircraft has its upper gun turret removed, to increase its speed. The Ju 188 bomber did not go into service in large numbers, but it made up an important part of the German bomber force during the attacks on England early in 1944 (Hans Altrogge).*

Ju 188E's. Later this leeway was made up, and many Ju 188A's were built.

In the early summer of 1943 Test Flight 188* received a number of initial production Ju 188's, and began service trials. The following August the type appeared over the British Isles for the first time. On the 18th of that month Second Lieutenant Hans Altrogge of I./K.G. 66 flew one of three Ju 188's which took part in an 88 aircraft attack on the Ruston and Hornsby works at Lincoln; the unsuccessful raid cost the Germans 11 bombers, though all the Ju 188's returned safely.

In the months that followed Ju 188's took a regular part in attacks on targets in Britain, and in minelaying operations off the coast. Typical of the latter were those on the nights of September 22 and 23, when Ju 188's of I./K.G. 66, operating from Soesterberg in Holland, marked the turning points and run-in points for other aircraft engaged in mining the Humber.

The similarity in wing shape and general layout between the Mosquito and the Ju 188 sometimes resulted in confusion between the two types, especially

*Erprobungskommando 188.*

The first protype of the Ju 188, showing the longer, pointed wing shape and the enlarged tail surfaces which distinguish this aircraft from the earlier Ju 88 (Gerhard Joos and I.W.M).

during night engagements. Altrogge recalls that when he first operated over Britain in the Junkers in 1943 searchlights would sometimes illuminate him then extinguish, night fighters would close in then break away without firing. As the Ju 188 became better known this immunity evaporated, but now the similarity caused the Mosquito crews some embarrassment. One amusing incident—if not so funny at the time—was when the commander of No. 488 Squadron Royal Air Force, Wing Commander R. C. Haine, was shot down while flying a Mosquito, in mistake for a Ju 188. During the subsequent inquiry the American P-61 Black Widow pilot was asked why he had opened fire; had he not been briefed that the Ju 188 was much larger than the Mosquito? "Well," the American solemnly replied in his Texas drawl, "Ah guess Ah must have thought that it was a *little* Junkers 188!"

## MARKING LONDON

At the beginning of 1944 the long awaited German bomber counter-offensive against Britain—Operation *Steinbock*—began. Two *Gruppen* with Ju 188's took part in these attacks, I./K.G. 66* and II./K.G. 2.

During *Steinbock* Major Helmut Schmidt's I./K.G. 66 operated in the pathfinder role. Typically, its Ju 188's would carry two 1,100 lb. high explosive bombs, plus 18 110 lb. LC 50 marker bombs; the latter burned with a distinctive white, green or yellow flame for about four minutes.

The first marking aircraft would arrive over the target at high level ten minutes before the main force was due, and release flares. Two minutes later further aircraft would go in at low level and plant their markers accurately in the light of the flares; this high-low procedure would continue until zero-hour for the main attack, more and more flares being dropped to guide in the bombers following.

During the attacks on the British capital I./K.G. 66, in common with other units, suffered heavy losses.

## TARGET BRISTOL

The operations against London continued until the spring of 1944, when the weight of the attacks shifted to other cities. The reader may get an idea of how these

*I./K.G. 66 also operated with Ju 88S's; see Volume One.

raids looked from the German side if one of them is described by one of the participants.

Leading Aircraftman* Rudi Prasse flew as navigator on a Ju 188A of the Second *Gruppe* of K.G. 2. His pilot was Sergeant Hans Engelke, and their aircraft bore the identification cypher U5 DP. Early on the morning of May 14, 1944, 91 German aircraft set out to bomb Bristol; U5 DP was one of them.

The briefing for the II./K.G. 2 crews took place in the operations room at Vannes on the evening of the 13th. The room resembled a small cinema, with folding benches on which the navigators had spread their charts; on the wall hung a large map of England. Prasses recalls.:

"The weather man† gives the known position: area weather, high level winds, weather at the target. I write it all down, note the wind, and work out my course.

"The weather man's monologue over, Captain Schroeder explains the operational orders: 'Co-ordinated attack on Bristol on May 14, attack time 0145 to 0150 hours. The first *Staffel* is to take off at 0010 hours. Crews are to take off so that they arrive at the target area five minutes before the attack time. K.G. 66 will do the target marking: double green sky markers, with full target illumination. All aircraft of our *Gruppe* have been loaded with high explosive bombs. Attack height 20,000 feet. And now the target. Please Mr. Boehm...'

"He moves to one side and the room is darkened. On the canvas screen is flashed an aerial photograph of Bristol. Captain Schroeder points out with his stick the various targets: an industrial works, a large barracks and the port area.

"I had been over Bristol once before, and knew that with those defences it would not be easy to bomb. With that weather—it was forecast as fine—there could be little doubt that the night fighters would be out in force."

Engelke and his crew left the briefing room shortly after 2100 hours, and changed into their flying kit. Then they made their way to the Junkers parked in its dispersal out on the airfield.

Loaded with two 2,200 and two 110 lb. bombs, U5

*Gefreiter

†Wetterfrosch—*weatherfrog in German aircrew slang.*

*The Ju 88B, with an all-glazed nose section and BWM 801 motors, came half way between the Ju 88 and the Ju 188. This sub-type did not go into production (I.W.M.).*

DP took off at 0030 hours. Prasse recalls:

"With its heavy load the machine was unwieldy. During the take-off I gripped the red emergency bomb jettison lever tightly, for the airfield was small and the obstruction lights were getting steadily closer."

However Engelke managed to lift the heavily-laden bomber off the ground in good time, and the Junkers

*Altrogge's Ju 188E, photographed inside its individual protective hangar at Montdidier in France (Hans Altrogge).*

"0045 hours! The first flares blossom in rows over the city, lighting the targets with a dazzling white light. Over them hang the rows of green sky markers, which float down slowly. On the ground the flak gunners concentrate their fire on the markers in an attempt to shoot them out. But it is too late. On the city heavy bombs are now bursting, and dark red fires rise into the sky.

"One short glance at the map—that must be the harbour there. I nudge Hans and point to the right: 'We will attack'.

"Bombdoors open, switches on!

"There is a small jerk as our bombs fall away.

"Bombdoors close!

*Major Helmut Schmidt commanded the Pathfinder unit I./K.G. 66 during Operation* Steinbock, *the air attacks on Britain in the early part of 1944.*

climbed away to the north. By 0110 hours the German crew was nearing the coast of England.

"20,000 feet. Now we climb at 600 feet per minute, with the airspeed steady at 310 m.p.h.* In front of us there emerges a dark outline: the English coast. There is nothing of the defences to be seen, the long arms of the searchlight beams do not grope out for us. But we know that now, ten minutes before the English coast, the enemy is getting ready for us. Now the first sirens are sounding in the coastal towns and on the airfields the first night fighters are already taking off. Hans begins to jink the aircraft—turning, climbing, diving—for nothing is more dangerous than holding a straight course for too long.

"As we cross the coast the first searchlight beams flash on; two, four, five beams grope after us, searching. Behind us are many more, certainly about 50: this is the famous English coastal searchlight

belt. Then we are through it, and it is dark again. Before us lies Bristol, our target.

"We arrive at the outskirts at 23,000 feet. Suddenly two great tentacles of light swing across the sky to flood the cabin with dazzling blue light, forcing us to screw up our blinded eyes. We are being coned by two searchlights, which now follow us. 'Put the jammer on'* shouts Hans. I hold my map against the nose so that the pilot can see his instruments. We dive through a thousand feet turning steeply to the left, then fly straight ahead. The two searchlights, which have been joined by a further two, hunt the sky for us but we are once more in the darkness. 'Heavy flak coming up' calls Erich (the ventral gunner), and Hans immediately changes course. There, above us at 26,000 feet the first eight shells burst.

"More searchlights cut across the sky, and the flak bursts multiply. The dance has begun! The pilot flies uncommonly well, improvising a regular aerobatic programme before our eyes.

"To the left and below us a flaming red torch goes down. I note in my log: 'Aircraft shot down at 0042 hours southwest of Bristol'.

*When Prasse described his flight he gave all these figures in German units, i.e. metres, kilometres per hour, metres per second, etc. These have been translated into British units in this account.

*The Ju 188 carried a Kettenhund radar jamming transmitter, to counter the British gunlaying and searchlight control radars.

*Above:* Two more photographs of Altrogge's aircraft. Note the balloon cable fend-off bar running round the nose section, and the way in which the fuselage cross is continued into the black under-surface in light grey *(Hans Altrogge).*

*Below and top of facing page:* Two pictures of Ju 188A's of K.G. 26, an anti-shipping unit. The type achieved little in this role *(Franz Selinger).*

*Right: Leading Aircraftsman Rudi Prasse flew as a navigator with the crew of a Ju 188A of II./K.G.2 during operation Steinbock. See "Target Bristol" (Rudi Prasse).*

"Our Dora, lighter by more than two tons, obeys its pilot and sweeps round in a steep left turn, on to a south easterly course away from the target. Soon we are clear".

The Junkers landed at Vannes at 0305 hours, without further incident.

From British records we know that the attack—which cost the *Luftwaffe* six bombers—was not so successful as it appeared to Prasse. Of the 83 tons of bombs recorded as having landed on British soil that night only a paltry three tons fell within the city limits of Bristol. The British fire decoy organisation had become extremely efficient by the spring of 1944 . . .

The *Steinbock* operations petered out at the end of May, and the units involved sat back to lick their wounds. But for the German bomber force in the west time was running out, for on June 6th Allied forces landed on the north coast of France. Again the tired and depleted *Gruppen* were thrown into action in the face of the strongest of defences. Again they suffered heavily.

As Ju 188 bombers were lost they had to be replaced by other types, for the last of these bombers had been delivered earlier in the year. By the autumn of 1944 the Ju 188 had virtually passed out of service as a bomber. It was to have been replaced in the front line

units by a progressive development with an improved high altitude performance, the Ju 388. But with the almost complete collapse of the German bomber arm in the summer of 1944, the Ju 388 never did see service with bomber units.

## SPECIFICATION JU 118A

**Crew**
Four.

**Power plant**
Two 1,776 h.p. Jumo 213A 12-cylinder in-line liquid cooled motors, mounted behind anular radiators.

**Dimensions**
Span: 72 ft. 2 in.; Length: 49 ft. 0½ in.; Wing area: 603 sq. ft.

**Weights**
Empty 21,825 lb.; Loaded 31,950 lb.

**Armament**
One 20 mm. cannon in the nose and another in the power-operated dorsal turret. One 13 mm. gun firing rearwards from the rear of the cabin; two 7·9 mm. guns firing rearwards from the underside of the cabin.

**Bomb load**
6,600 lb.

**Maximum speed**
323 m.p.h.

**Maximum range**
1,500 miles (with 3,300 lb. of bombs).

**Service ceiling**
33,000 ft.

# The Mistletoe

During the Second World War both sides produced freak weapons, weapons tailored to destroy a specific type of target. From the British side came Barnes Wallis' bouncing bomb, built specially for the single attack on the German dams. The German equivalent to the dam-busting weapon, in terms of imaginative

A Mistletoe 2 of K.G. 30 under camouflage netting at Oranienburg early in 1945, one of the combinations earmarked for the "Iron Hammer" operation. Note the short stand-off probe fitted to the front of the hollow charge warhead, and the four crush fuses at the tip. The Luftwaffe planners expected great things from the Mistletoe in action, but in the event it achieved little (Hanfried Schliephake).

The idea of mounting transport gliders rigidly below powered aircraft was tested in 1942, using a Bf 109 fighter and a DFS 230 glider (Franz Selinger).

design and specialized destructive power, was the Mistletoe* device.

It was in 1942 that the German Glider Research Institute† started trials with a novel method of getting gliders airborne. Instead of the more usual arrangement of the glider being towed behind the aircraft, test pilot Fritz Stamer initiated a series of trials in which the glider was rigidly mounted *underneath* the powered aircraft. The feasibility of the pick-a-back scheme was proved using, amongst other combinations, the Klemm KL35B and the DFS 230 glider.

Early in 1943 the idea took on a new form: a piloted Bf 109 fighter mounted on top of an unmanned explosive-laden Ju 88 bomber by means of supporting struts. This was the Mistletoe. The pilot in the upper

*Mistel.

†*Deutsches Forschungsinstitut für Segelflug.*

### THE MISLETOE ATTACK

A. *"Pop-up" from low level to 2,500 feet; low level approach made to avoid defensive radar cover.*

B. *Level out at 2,500 feet, two and a half miles from target; pilot aligns the combination on his target.*

C. *Range one and a half miles, pilot pushes the combination into a dive.*

D. *Elevation alignment on target, angle of dive 15 degrees.*

E. *Range one mile; pilot releases lower explosive component, climbs away steeply to get clear.*

F. *Explosive lower component maintains previous flight path, under control of the autopilot, to impact with the target.*

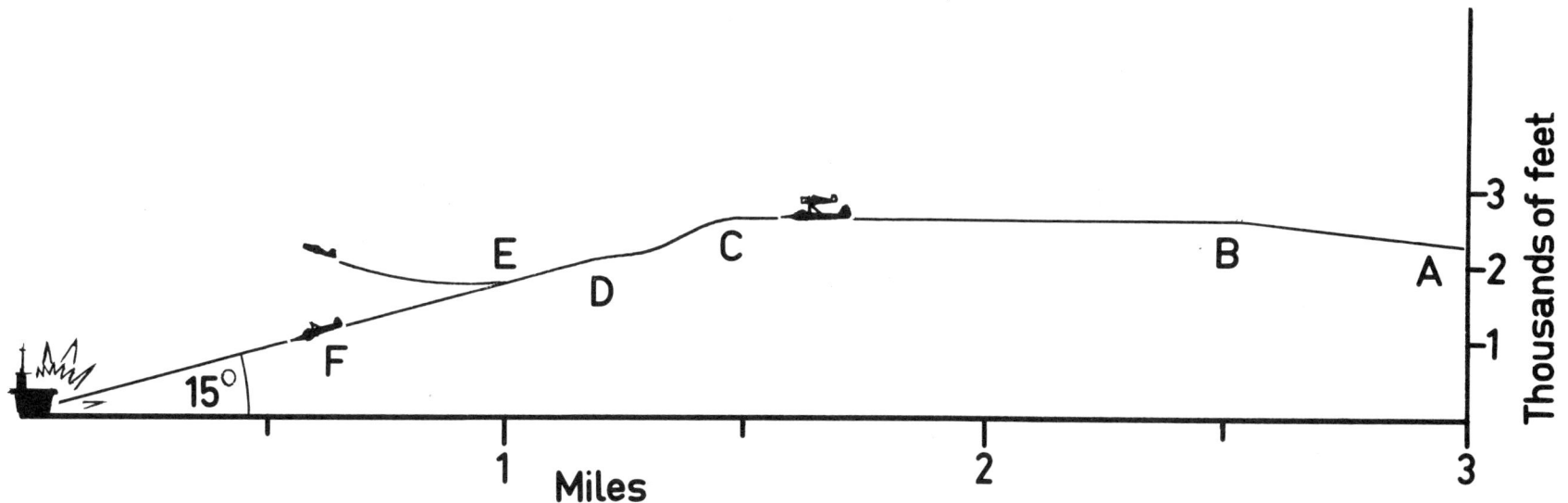

## THE MISTLETOE ATTACK

machine was to control the combination; when he got to the target he would put the combination into a 15 degree descent and aim the whole lot at the target. At a range of about three quarters of a mile from the objective he was to separate his fighter from the lower component and climb away, leaving the latter to fly straight on under control of the automatic pilot until it impacted. The fighter pilot was then to return to base in the normal way.

Thus far the Mistletoe idea had little to commend it, for the expenditure of one Ju 88 bomber to deliver a mere 3½ ton warhead to a target was a grossly uneconomical method. But if a special warhead could be fitted to the explosive aircraft, a warhead which could punch through almost any protective layer of armour, that was a different matter altogether.

*A test flight of an early Mistletoe 1, showing the machines on the ground, airborne, and immediately after separating. The Bf 109 pilot has pulled his aircraft up sharply after release, to ensure a clean break (via E. Creek).*

# THE HOLLOW CHARGE

The warhead fitted to the Mistletoe was of the hollow charge type. Such warheads, fired from Bazooka-type weapons, were used a great deal during the war against tanks. But with the Mistletoe a hollow charge warhead weighing 7,700 pounds—far larger than any built before or since—was to be used.

The hollow charge, as fitted to the Mistletoe, was intended to blow a hole through the thick steel armour of a battleship. The shape of the 3,800 pound explosive charge was important, and was as shown in the diagram (A). At the front end of the explosive charge was a cone-shaped hollow cavity which was lined with a layer of soft metal—either copper or aluminium. It was important that a soft metal be used for this liner, since a harder metal would prevent the hollow charge action from developing properly. Four electrical crush fuses, for firing the detonator of the main charge, were mounted at the end of the nine foot long stand-off probe which protruded from the front of the warhead; the detonator for the main charge was situated at the rear of the warhead.

When the stand-off probe hit the target (B) the crush fuses operated, set off the detonator, and thus fired the main charge. Because of its shape and the fact that it was burning from the rear forwards, the force of the main charge was focused on to the soft metal liner. The liner became fluid, and was pushed forward from the centre of the cone in a fine jet.

A split-second later (C) the hollow charge action had developed completely. The metal in the liner was now "squirted" forwards in a stream about one foot in diameter, a stream which reached speeds of between 20 and 25 times the speed of sound*. Thus the hollow-charge acted as a "gun", and the soft metal liner as a "bullet". The colossal speed attained by the thin jet of soft metal gave it the energy necessary to "drill" a hole clean through steel armour with a thickness of up to four times the maximum diameter

*An early Mistletoe 1 combination, with the hollow charge warhead fitted in place of the crew compartment of the Ju 88 lower component. This warhead was capable of "drilling" a hole clean through the hull of even the most heavily armoured warship.*

*15,000 to 19,000 miles per hour.

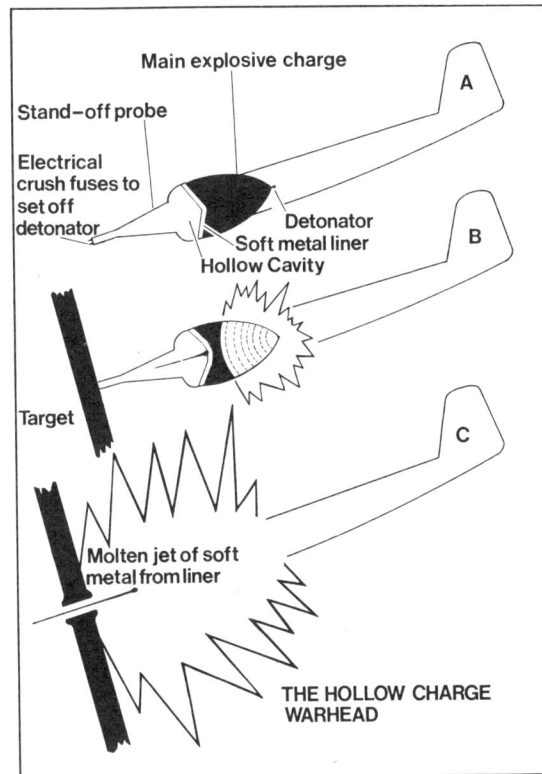

Main explosive charge
Stand–off probe
Electrical crush fuses to set off detonator
Detonator
Soft metal liner
Hollow Cavity
Target
Molten jet of soft metal from liner

THE HOLLOW CHARGE WARHEAD

of the warhead itself; in the case of the six foot diameter warhead fitted to the Mistletoe lower component, this gave a theoretical maximum penetration of the order of 24 feet. Such a warhead would penetrate the heaviest armour carried by a ship with ease. Once through the outer protective shell of the target, and now confined inside it, the jet of high energy metal would cause a "dreadful mess", vaporizing anything in its path.

The stand-off probe was necessary to set off the main explosive charge at the optimum distance from the target, so that the soft metal liner had time to form itself into a thin jet before it struck. Within limits, the further the charge from the target when it was detonated, the thinner and deeper the hole "drilled"; the closer the charge to the target, the wider and shallower the penetration. Both long and short stand-off probes were used with the Mistletoe. The entire hollow-charge action took place within one ten-thousandth part of a second, during which time a relatively slow-moving Ju 88 explosive aircraft, impacting at 400 m.p.h., moved forwards about a

half an inch. This, then, was the potential of the Mistletoe device.

The Ju 88 lower components had their crew compartments removed at the after bulkhead, then these were re-fitted in place by means of quick-release fasteners. For ferry and training flights both the upper and the lower components were manned. At the last possible moment before an attack, the crew compartment was removed for the last time and the deadly hollow-charge warhead fitted in its place. This task required six mechanics, two armourers, and "a crane able to lift four tons", and took one day. The act had an air of finality about it, for once the warhead-fitted Mistletoe had taken off the fighter pilot could not land the combination; whether it reached the target or not, the Ju 88 lower component was doomed. A series of aiming tests against cliffs on the Danish island of Moen proved the feasibility of the weapon.

Mistletoe pilots began training in April 1944, using the first two prototypes. Each man completed ten flights without releasing the lower component, then three flights each with a release. The pilots found that the poor view forwards from the fighter cockpit made the initial part of the take-off run difficult, and this

*This interesting photograph shows six Mistletoe combinations being readied for action. Since the hollow charge warheads were fitted only shortly before a specific attack was to be mounted, such group photographs are extremely rare. Almost certainly this picture was taken at St Dizier in France, immediately prior to the attack on the Allied invasion fleet.*

ruled out the possibility of night take-offs. However, once it was airborne they found the Mistletoe easy to fly, if a little sluggish on the controls.

Mistletoe combinations were put together using a number of different types. The original employed the Bf 109F and the Ju 88A, later ones employed various sub-types of the Fw 190 and the Ju 88. Versions projected but never assembled comprised an Me 262 jet fighter on top of a Ju 287 jet bomber, and an He 162 jet fighter mounted on an Arado E 377A flying bomb*.

## THE SCAPA FLOW ATTACK PLAN

In April 1944 the Mistletoe was judged ready for service use, and the first 15 conversions—all Bf 109's

*The E377A was constructed specially for use as a Mistletoe explosive component.*

on Ju 88A's—were ordered for mid-June. The weapon was to be used against battleships and aircraft carriers in harbour, and initial plans for such an attack were laid.

On the April 16, 1944 the Operations Staff of the *Luftwaffe* completed its top secret paper "The Operational Possibilities of the Mistletoe". In the paper three major fleet anchorages were considered for attack: Gibraltar, Leningrad and Scapa Flow. Of these Gibraltar was the most difficult, for the target was 850 miles from the nearest German base in France; at this extreme range the pilot would have to crash land in Spain after the mission, for there would be no fuel left to get him back to France. Even accepting the need for a one-way trip, the distance was so great that the attack was not feasible unless the aircraft could cross Spanish territory to get to the target; however, as the plan stressed ". . . the Fuehrer has always refused to give his permission for this." Leningrad was ruled out because of the difficulties of achieving a measure of surprise so vital for a successful attack; and in any case, the Russian ships there were effectively bottled up in the Baltic. That left only Scapa Flow.

The airfield at Grove in central Denmark was

Junkers Ju 188E, flown by Second Lieutenant Hans Altrogge, of I. Gruppe, Kampfgeschwader 66, during the winter 1943/44. This unit operated over Britain in the pathfinder role, from Montdidier, Rennes and Chartres in France.

*The remaining views will be found overleaf.*

Junkers Ju 188E.

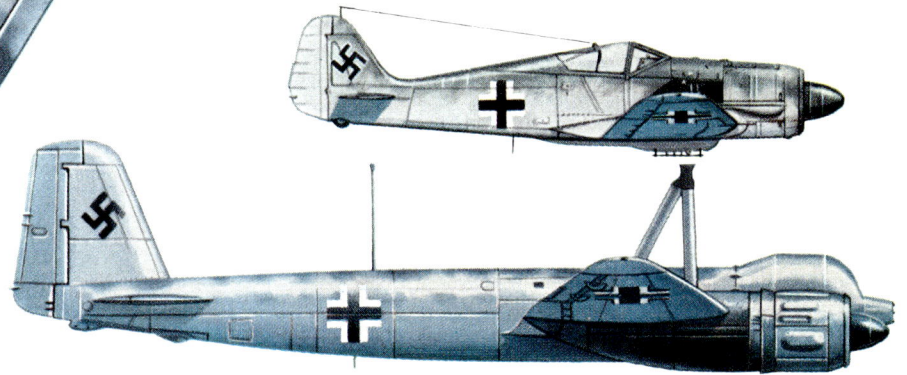

Mistletoe 2 employed against the bridge over the Oder at Kuestrin, during the attack on the 12th April 1945.

*The remaining views will be found overleaf.*

Mistletoe 2.

selected as being the most suitable for the attack on Scapa Flow, 480 miles away. The paper warned:

"In the target area the very strongest of defences may be expected. Exactly how strong is not known, for our radio monitoring service is not effective north of The Wash. However, Department Ic* estimates that on the airfields between the Firth of Forth and the north of Scotland there are 160 to 200 aircraft of the types Spitfire, Hurricane, Mosquito and Beaufighter. In addition, there is a belt of radar stations giving gap-free cover out to sea. . . ."

A fighter escort over the target was out of the question since the nearest *Luftwaffe* airfield to Scapa, at Stavanger in Norway, was still 350 miles away.

*Intelligence.

*Close-up of the supporting struts: (a) The port main supporting leg, showing the control connections going down to the lower component; (b) the starboard main supporting leg, showing the pull-away electrical connectors and the pipe to carry fuel from the lower to the upper component during the outward flight; (c) the "V" strut supporting legs fitted to the upper fuselage of the Ju 88, showing the electrical cabling and the fuel pipe; (d) the supporting strut from the wing of the Ju 88; . . . see over page . . . and . . .*

a

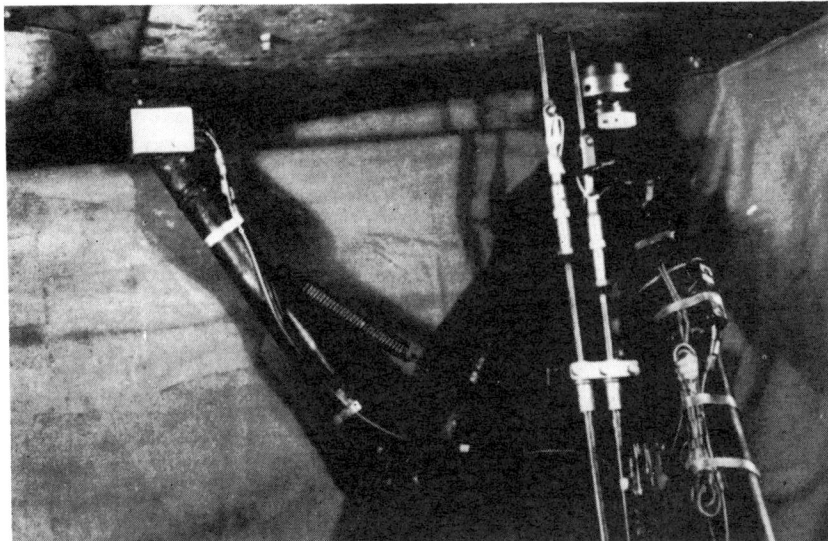

b

c

d

... the tail supporting strut.

prior to the attack. The Mistletoe pilots would have no time to orbit Scapa Flow while they sought out their targets; each man would have to have an aerial photograph with the exact position of his own target marked on it. To assist the pilots to navigate accurately, a series of Swan radio buoys* was to be laid out across the North Sea immediately prior to the attack. These buoys were shaped like an ordinary bomb, but when they were dropped into the sea from an aircraft they floated on the surface and emitted radio signals on which other aircraft could home. For an aircraft flying at 600 feet the Swan radio beacon had a range of about 60 miles; so during their approach flights the Mistletoe pilots were to "beacon crawl" across the North Sea to Scapa Flow.

It is impossible to do more than speculate on how successful the planned Mistletoe attack on Scapa Flow might have been, always assuming that the unwieldy combinations would have been able to sneak through the powerful defences. The big ships of the Home Fleet were continuously coming and going, and the

*Funkboje Schwan.

number at the anchorage varied a great deal during the summer of 1944. During June and July, for example, the fleet aircraft carriers *Victorious, Indomitable* and *Implacable, Indefatigable, Formidable* and *Furious* all put in an appearance at Scapa Flow, as did the battleships *Duke of York* and *Howe.* So had the attack been launched at a time when the anchorage was full, there would have been targets in plenty. And we have already seen how potent the Mistletoe was.

## IN ACTION

The first unit to receive the Mistletoe was the Second *Staffel* of K.G. 101, commanded by Captain Horst Rudat. But before Rudat could move his *Staffel* to Grove things had come to the boil in France, for on the June 6 Allied forces had landed in Normandy. Accordingly, the few Mistletoe combinations available were ferried to St Dizier in France, for operations against the invasion fleet. The Mistletoe pilots did claim some hits, but none of these are confirmed in Allied records. An explanation for this could be that some of the hits were on the old French battleship *Courbet,* which was being used as a blockship for the

Because of the difficulties of take-off and aiming the Mistletoe in the face of strong defences, a night or bad weather attack was judged to be "impossible". The strike was planned for dusk.

The only hope for a successful attack was if the element of surprise could be exploited. The German pilots were to cross the North Sea flying as low as they could, but certainly below 600 feet, so as to keep below the cover of the British radar sets for as long as possible. At the last moment they were to climb to about 3,000 feet, then go straight into their attack runs.

There were two essential pre-requisites for such a straight-in attack: reliable Intelligence on the position of the targets, and very accurate navigation. The paper stressed the need for the most careful reconnaissance

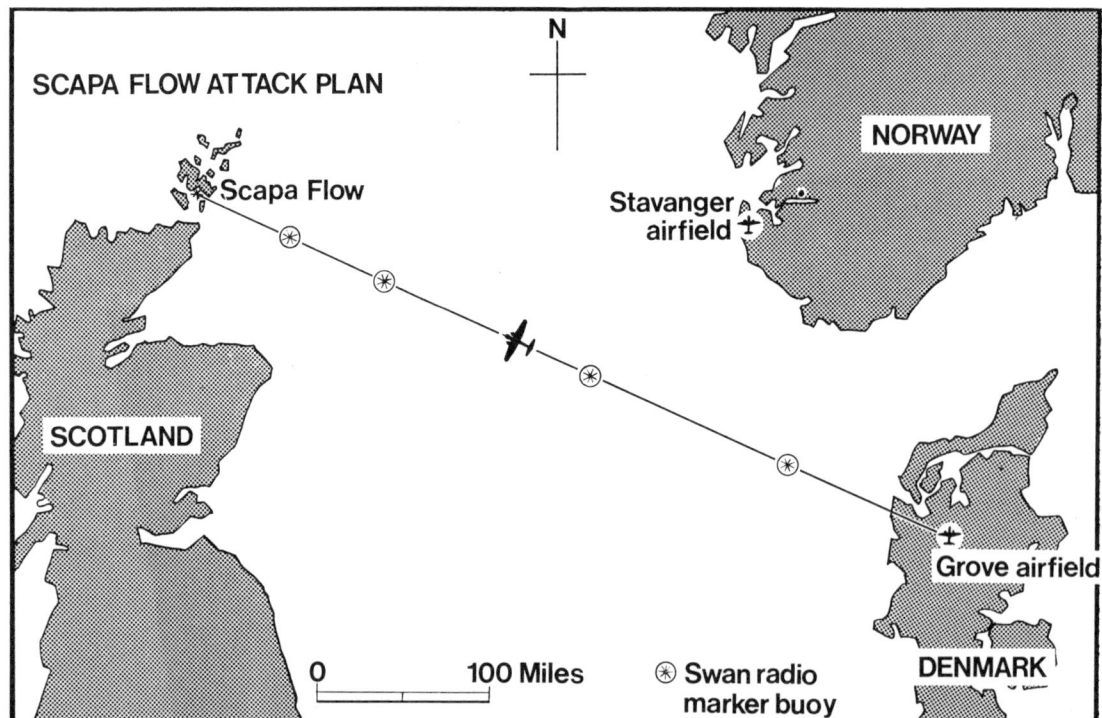

SCAPA FLOW ATTACK PLAN

N

NORWAY

Scapa Flow

Stavanger airfield

SCOTLAND

Grove airfield

DENMARK

0     100 Miles

⊛ Swan radio marker buoy

British "Mulberry" harbour at Courseulles. Since the ship was already lying on the sea bottom, in shallow water, the Royal Navy were more than happy to have the Germans attack her in preference to more worthwhile targets. So *Courbet* was dressed up to look as conspicuous as possible, with an enormous tricolour with the cross of Louraine; thereafter she acted as a magnet for attacks. She certainly collected several bombs and torpedoes, and possibly a Mistletoe or two.

In the autumn of 1944 the plan for the Mistletoe attack on Scapa Flow was again pressed forward, and composites flew into Grove and neighbouring Danish airfields in readiness. But the Royal Air Force struck first, and set in train a pattern of events which brought the carefully-laid German plan to nothing.

On the November 11, 1944 Lancasters attacked the German battleship *Tirpitz* with 12,000 pound Tallboy bombs, and caused her to capsize. With *Tirpitz* out of the way there was no call for battleships or fleet aircraft carriers to be held in the Atlantic, and within weeks those which had served with the Home Fleet at Scapa Flow were on their way to the Pacific. So before the plan could be put into effect all the worthwhile targets had left Scapa Flow. The combinations would have to be used elsewhere.

## THE "IRON HAMMER" PLAN

"Operation Iron Hammer"*, the planned blow to knock-out the Russian armament industry, had first been mooted at the end of 1943. The key targets in the production complex round Moscow and Gorky were judged to be the steam and hydro-electric generating stations; it was known that the Russians lacked the plant to produce such turbines—most of the equipment scheduled for attack under the "Iron Hammer" plan had been supplied by the Germans before the war. As a result the *Luftwaffe* planners felt that the Russians would not be able to effect repairs for a very long time. But the plan could not be carried through because the re-training of the units taking part had not been completed by March 1944, when the Russians overran the advanced bases which were to have been used. Now the targets lay beyond the range of the He 111.

The idea of the knock-out blow was revived in December 1944, when the plan was expanded in scope and re-scheduled for the spring of 1945 this time using Mistletoe combinations. The operation's supporters believed that such a powerful blow from the supposedly dying German Air Force would come as a great shock to the Russians, and might well have the useful

secondary effect of causing them to pull back fighter units for home defence.

Despite the deep penetration necessary to reach the "Iron Hammer" targets, the German planning staff felt that the operation had a good chance of success. Since the autumn of 1943 German bomber activity over rear areas in the east had been negligible, and as a result the Russian home air defences were weak and underdeveloped. The only German unit to fly regular

*Second Lieutenant Hans Altrogge of I./K.G. 66 flew a Ju 188 as pathfinder during the Mistletoe attack on the bridge over the Oder at Kuestrin on the 12th April 1945 (Hans Altrogge).*

missions over Russia since then had been *Kampfgeschwader* 200, which was engaged in dropping and supplying agents. The unit's aircraft had regularly carried radar observers, and as a result the Germans knew that the radar cover in the rear areas was thin. Since the targets were both large and ill-defended, a night attack using flares was judged feasible.

For the operation specially modified Mistletoe combinations were prepared, able to cover the 760 mile distance from the base airfields to the targets. The Fw 190 upper components were each to carry two drop tanks for fuel, and additional tanks for both fuel and oil. Following tests held at Udetfeld with the warhead, it was calculated that two hits with hollow-charge fitted Ju 88's would be sufficient against the smaller power stations, while six hits would be necessary against the larger ones.

The revived plan had intended that the Mistletoe combinations should take off from airfields in East Prussia; later, as the front line had moved back with disconcerting speed during the Russian offensives in January and February, 1945, the operation was re-planned to use airfields at Oranienburg, Parchim, Laertz, Marienehe and Peenemuende. The return flights were to be either to the home bases or else to airfields in the Courland Peninsular pocket*, depending upon fuel and weather conditions.

Lieutenant Colonel Werner Baumbach was made responsible for the execution of the Iron Hammer operation. Under his control were the Mistletoe combinations of K.G. 30 and K.G. 200, as well as a number of He 111's, Ju 88's and Ju 290's which were to act as route and target markers during the attack.

However, by the time sufficient Mistletoe combinations were available, there were other tasks for which they could be used. For by March, 1945, the Russians were streaming westwards over the Vistula bridges. Something of the dilemma that faced the Germans may be sensed from a conversation held between Hitler and General Karl Koller, the Chief of Staff of the *Luftwaffe*, on March 26, 1945:

Koller: Altogether there are 82 Mistletoe combinations ready for use. If the urgent attacks on the Vistula bridges are carried out as you, my Fuehrer, have commanded Lieutenant Colonel Baumbach, there will remain 56 combinations for the "Iron Hammer" operation. Since the report from General Christian would you not prefer that we carry through a smaller "Iron Hammer" with these 56

*Unternehmen Eisenhammer.*

*The Courland Peninsula, in northern Lithuania, had been cut off since the summer of 1944, but was to hold out until the end of the war.*

Mistletoes? I wish to propose that as well as the urgent Vistula bridge attacks, the "Iron Hammer" operation should be carried through with these 56 Mistletoe combinations. The attack on the Gorki group of targets would then have to be omitted. We should then knock out 80 per-cent of their electrical generating capacity; of their 1,094 million killowatts the reduction would be only 378 million killowatts. I ask therefore that the proposed "Iron Hammer" operation be approved; technically we can be completely ready by the 28th/29th, provided the weather conditions are favourable.

Hitler: I do not wish to divide the effort, because when we do it a second time the enemy will be ready, and will reply with strong defensive measures.

Koller: Naturally it would be a shame if the complete "Iron Hammer" operation could not be flown, but I do not know when we could ever do it again; the earliest that it could be done again is during the next moon period. I should also like to believe that the range of the targets is such that strong defences will not be met, because presumably the enemy will not expect us to attack over such great distances.

Hitler: Nevertheless, one knows how significant it would have been if the enemy had attacked our power stations simultaneously. It is exactly the same with the enemy. For the present I prefer to give up the Vistula bridge attacks; that can be done later.

Koller: So the "Iron Hammer" operation can be carried out in full with no diversion of effort for the Vistula bridge attacks?

The transcript ended: "The Fuehrer agreed with this."

But the "Iron Hammer" operation was not to be mounted on the March 28. Shortly after the conversation it became clear that the bridge attacks could not be "done later". The Russians were massing for a

*When the war ended the majority of the Mistletoe combinations assembled for the "Iron Hammer" attack were captured on the ground by the victorious Allied troops (U.S.A.F.).*

breakthrough along the line of the Oder River where for the time being they were held, though in places less than 35 miles from Berlin itself. At Kuestrin they had already established a bridgehead on the west bank which had resisted all German attempts to throw it back. When the Russian attack came, there could be no doubt that the crossings at Kuestrin would play a major part in it; accordingly, the carefully husbanded stock of Mistletoe combinations was sent in to smash them.

## THE ODER BRIDGE ATTACKS

In charge of the Oder bridge attacks was Colonel Hans-Joachim Helbig. This use of Mistletoe combinations against bridges was a measure of desperation, for although they were potentially a very effective weapons against ships or concrete buildings whose walls would contain some of the force of the explosion, they were quite unsuitable for this task. Not only was the accuracy of the Mistletoe inadequate for use

against such long narrow targets, but the specialized warheads merely blew holes *through* the bridges without damaging any vital part of the structure.

Typical of the attacks on the bridges at Kuestrin was that on April 12, 1945. At 1825 hours that evening Second Lieutenant Hans Altrogge took off from Peenemuende in a Ju 88 of I./K.G. 66, to act as lead aircraft for the attack. Four Mistletoe combinations followed him into the air, and the curious formation headed south towards the target. The view from the upper component Fw 190's was not good, and the Ju 88 pathfinder flew some two miles in front and 1,500 feet above the combinations, so as to stay in sight. It was dusk when Altrogge arrived at Kuestrin. When overhead the bridges he rocked his wings then climbed away: this was the cue for the Mistletoe pilots to push their aircraft down and go straight into the attack. In the face of heavy anti-aircraft fire the pilots pressed home their dives, separated, then pulled away. The salvo of explosive Ju 88's continued on, and from his vantage point Altrogge watched the bridges disappear in a cloud of smoke, mud and spray. Freed of their burdens the Fw 190's became potent fighters once again, and now vengefully curved in to "work over" the flak pits which had made things so hot for them during the attack run.

Before the smoke cleared it was dark, and Altrogge was unable to observe the results of the strike. But from Russian records we know that the bridges continued in use after the attack. The Kuestrin bridges were of the simple pontoon type, erected by Soviet army engineers; pontoons are easy to replace.

The Russians launched their great offensive on April 16, and within two days had forced two bridgeheads, one 20 miles wide and one 30 miles wide, on the western bank of the Oder. More and more pontoon bridges were thrown across the river, and the *Luftwaffe* used everything it had, including Mistletoes and Hs 293 glider bombs, in an attempt to smash them. But such was the force of the Russian push that even when some of the crossings were temporarily put out of action the drive was not slackened in the least.

When the war ended, in May 1945, the Mistletoe had achieved none of its spectacular promise. *Potentially* the weapon was capable of a great deal. For example, had a dozen or so combinations penetrated the defences and reached the anchorage at Scapa Flow, they could well have disabled the entire battleship and aircraft carrier strength of the British Home Fleet. Had such a blow been synchronised with a sortie by the German battleship *Tirpitz*—assuming that *Tirpitz* could have been made serviceable following the damaging attacks by aircraft and midget

submarines—severe disruption to Britain's Atlantic lifeline might have resulted. But by the middle of September 1944 it was already too late. Then the cumulative damage suffered by *Tirpitz* had rendered her unfit for sea; she was retained in service merely to keep Allied warships tied down. A successful Mistletoe attack in November 1944 would have inflicted a severe blow on British morale, but would have achieved little else; the battleships and fleet carriers of the Home Fleet took no part in the closing months of the European war anyway. So when the Mistletoe was ready for action in sufficient numbers, the important issues had already been decided.

It was the same with the "Iron Hammer" plan. Had the operation been successfully mounted in 1944 the mighty Russian advance might well have been forced to a halt for want of supplies. But by the early part of 1945 it was too late for such an attack to make much impression: the Russian forces could have continued on pretty much as they did, using munitions already manufactured.

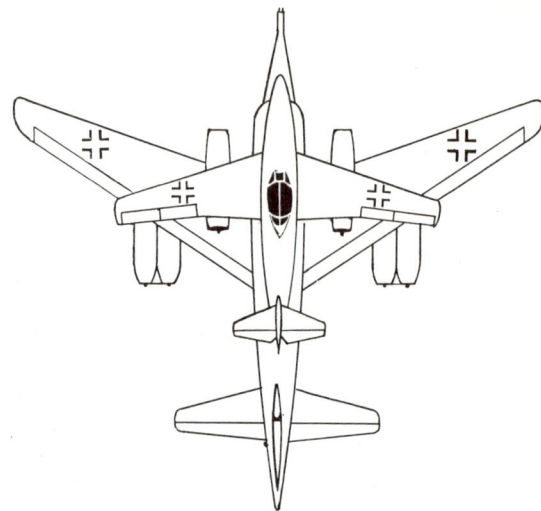

*The Mistletoe 4 was to have comprised an Me 262B upper component, and a Ju 287 swept-forward wing bomber as the lower component. It never progressed beyond the drawing board.*

## MISTLETOE VARIANTS

Mistletoe 1 Ju 88A-4 and Bf 109F-4.
Mistletoe 2 Ju 88G-1 and Fw 190A-8 or F-8.
Mistletoe 3A Ju 88A-4 and Fw 190A-8.
Mistletoe 3B Ju 88H-4 and Fw 190A-8.
Mistletoe 3C Ju 88G-10 and Fw 190F-8.
Mistletoe 4 Ju 287 and Me 262.
Mistletoe 5 Arado E 377A and He 162.
*Main additional components fitted during conversion to the Mistletoe role:*
Patin three-axis autopilot, as modified by Junkers, to the Ju 88.
Zeise optical sight, to the upper component.
Connecting frame, to the lower component.
Additional engine instruments mounted on the outside of the engines of the lower component, so that the pilot above could observe engine temperatures, boost pressures, etc.
7,800 pound hollow-charge warhead, containing 3,800 pounds of explosive (70 per-cent hexogen and 30 per-cent TNT). Impact fused, arming took place about three seconds after separation.

## SPECIFICATION MISTLETOE 1

**Crew**
One.

**Weight**

| | |
|---|---|
| Fully loaded Bf 109, modified as control aircraft | 6,200 lb. |
| Fully loaded Ju 88, modified as explosive aircraft | 26,500 lb. |
| Combination | 32,700 lb. |

Separation of fighter took place at between 1,000 and 3,000 yards from the target, at a dive angle of between 10 and 20 degrees.

**Speed of impact (explosive component):**
370 m.p.h.

**Radius of action**
480 miles (fighter uses fuel from the lower component during the outward flight, returns on the internal fuel it carries plus that in the 66 gallon drop tank).

**Performance of the combination**
Maximum speed 300 m.p.h., cruising speed 270 m.p.h.